Beth Buckley

Talk and Learning

Attitudes to Speaking, Listening and Collaborative Work and the Quality of Children's Talk

VDM Verlag Dr. Müller

Impressum/Imprint (nur für Deutschland/ only for Germany)
Bibliografische Information der Deutschen Nationalbibliothek: Die Deutsche Nationalbibliothek
verzeichnet diese Publikation in der Deutschen Nationalbibliografie; detaillierte bibliografische
Daten sind im Internet über http://dnb.d-nb.de abrufbar.
Alle in diesem Buch genannten Marken und Produktnamen unterliegen warenzeichen-, marken-
oder patentrechtlichem Schutz bzw. sind Warenzeichen oder eingetragene Warenzeichen der
jeweiligen Inhaber. Die Wiedergabe von Marken, Produktnamen, Gebrauchsnamen,
Handelsnamen, Warenbezeichnungen u.s.w. in diesem Werk berechtigt auch ohne besondere
Kennzeichnung nicht zu der Annahme, dass solche Namen im Sinne der Warenzeichen- und
Markenschutzgesetzgebung als frei zu betrachten wären und daher von jedermann benutzt
werden dürften.

Coverbild: www.purestockx.com

Verlag: VDM Verlag Dr. Müller Aktiengesellschaft & Co. KG
Dudweiler Landstr. 99, 66123 Saarbrücken, Deutschland
Telefon +49 681 9100-698, Telefax +49 681 9100-988, Email: info@vdm-verlag.de
Zugl.: Liverpool, John Moores University, Masters Dissertation, 2006

Herstellung in Deutschland:
Schaltungsdienst Lange o.H.G., Berlin
Books on Demand GmbH, Norderstedt
Reha GmbH, Saarbrücken
Amazon Distribution GmbH, Leipzig
ISBN: 978-3-639-12613-6

Imprint (only for USA, GB)
Bibliographic information published by the Deutsche Nationalbibliothek: The Deutsche
Nationalbibliothek lists this publication in the Deutsche Nationalbibliografie; detailed
bibliographic data are available in the Internet at http://dnb.d-nb.de.
Any brand names and product names mentioned in this book are subject to trademark, brand or
patent protection and are trademarks or registered trademarks of their respective holders. The use
of brand names, product names, common names, trade names, product descriptions etc. even
without a particular marking in this works is in no way to be construed to mean that such names
may be regarded as unrestricted in respect of trademark and brand protection legislation and
could thus be used by anyone.

Cover image: www.purestockx.com

Publisher:
VDM Verlag Dr. Müller Aktiengesellschaft & Co. KG
Dudweiler Landstr. 99, 66123 Saarbrücken, Germany
Phone +49 681 9100-698, Fax +49 681 9100-988, Email: info@vdm-publishing.com
Liverpool, John Moores University, Masters Dissertation, 2006

Printed in the U.S.A.
Printed in the U.K. by (see last page)
ISBN: 978-3-639-12613-6

Acknowledgements

I wish to thank my supervisor, Kate Johnston, for all her guidance and feedback throughout this research project. I am also extremely grateful to Dr John Harrison for helping to edit my lengthy drafts. I would also like to thank my brother-in-law, David, for reading and commenting on my final draft. Thanks to my husband, John, for his moral and technical support and to my Dad for his encouragement. Finally, my thanks go to the staff and children who took part in this research project.

List of Acronyms or Abbreviations	
CPD	Continuing Professional Development
DfEE	Department for Education and Employment
DfES	Department for Education and Skills
EAZ	Education Action Zone
FFT	Framework for Teaching
FSG	Foundation Stage Guidance
ICT	Information and Communication Technology
INSET	In Service Training
KS1	Key Stage 1 (Infants)
KS2	Key Stage 2 (Juniors)
KS3	Key Stage 3 (Years 7, 8 and 9 in Secondary)
LEA	Local Education Authority
LA	Local Authority
NC	National Curriculum
NLS	National Literacy Strategy
NLS FFT	National Literacy Strategy Framework for Teaching
NNS	National Numeracy Strategy
NQT	Newly Qualified Teacher
OfSTED	Office for Standards in Education
PNS	Primary National Strategy
QCA	Qualifications and Curriculum Authority
QTS	Qualified Teacher Status
TTA	Teacher Training Agency
TDA	Teacher Development Agency

Table of Contents		page
	List of Acronyms or Abbreviations	p2
	Aim and Objectives	p4
Chapter One	Introduction and Rationale for Research Project	p5
Chapter Two	Literature Review and Context for Research	p7
Chapter Three	Methodology and Research Activity	p26
Chapter Four	Findings and Discussion of Results ~ Pupil and Teacher Data	p38
Chapter Five	Findings and Discussion of Results ~ Discourse Analysis Data	p57
Chapter Six	Reflections on the Research Process, Conclusions and Recommendations	p80
	Appendices Appendix A ~ School Correspondence (not included, as confidential) Appendix B ~ School Proformas (blank) Appendix C ~ Methodology Appendix D ~ Transcripts Appendix E ~ Charts, Tables and Other Data	p89 p 90 p 96 p 97 p158
	Bibliography	p163

An Investigation into the Opportunities for
Peer Group Talk and Collaboration
in the Primary Classroom.

Aim:

To investigate the relationship between peer talk, collaborative work and learning.

Objectives:

- To identify the opportunities that pupils have to work collaboratively through talk.

- To analyse the types and quality of talk.

- To investigate whether opportunities for paired or group talk support or hinder task completion.

- To look for evidence of pupils scaffolding each other's learning.

- To explore pupils' and teachers' attitudes to paired and group talk.

Chapter One: Introduction and Rationale for Research Project

Before examining the literature, I will outline the rationale for my research study. As a primary teacher, I had used peer talk (mainly paired but some groups) to further children's learning, by enabling them to share ideas, interact and work collaboratively. Observations suggested it gave children confidence; feeling less worried about what to say and write. Working collaboratively appeared to help them internalise their learning. At the time I did not know the theoretical underpinnings of why peer talk was so effective.

As a Literacy Consultant, I was concerned by the lack of opportunity teachers gave to children for paired talk or group activities. A key part of my role was demonstrating and then team teaching peer talk. In my experience, teachers were surprised by how quickly children benefited from this strategy. Adults often share ideas with colleagues to produce better results than just working alone. Mercer (2000, p.2) illustrates this point, using an example of three people solving a crossword puzzle, because each brought different experiences and knowledge.

My understanding of talk changed through studying the Open University Course: *Language and Literacy in a Changing World*. This inspired me to look at talk more closely, both in terms of analysing my own teaching practice, and as a Literacy Consultant, observing and monitoring other people's teaching. During a research project undertaken during my OU studies, I observed an effective example of peer scaffolding, where two boys were asked to play 'The Entertainer'. One boy, who had more musical experience, supports the other boy's learning, by demonstrating how to play both parts and then instructing his peer to practise more slowly until the piece was mastered.

The above-mentioned small-scale research project, undertaken in my previous role as Literacy Consultant, gave me more impetus for this research project. My initial readings of research had indicated why effective language skills and peer interaction were crucial in learning. It inspired me to investigate the extent to which this was happening in one secondary school in my Education Action Zone. I tracked a year 7 class for several days, observing children in all subjects, with a variety of teachers. I identified opportunities for children to talk to each other when doing work tasks and then evaluated the quality of such interactions. My findings showed there were limited opportunities for peer talk in the lessons observed; the majority of talk came from the teachers.

I have concluded that neither the 1998 *National Literacy Strategy* (NLS) nor the 1999 *National Numeracy Strategy* (NNS) give enough importance to speaking and listening. The 1999 *National Curriculum* (NC) for English has three elements: speaking and listening; reading; and writing, but the *National Literacy Strategy* only has explicit objectives for reading and writing; with speaking and listening only being implicit. Attempts to redress the balance have been made, to some extent, with the publication of: *Speaking, Listening, Learning: working with children in Key Stages 1 and 2 (QCA, 2003b)*, which teachers can utilise along with the NLS. For teaching and learning in the Early Years, the profile of oracy has been raised with the advent of the *Foundation Stage Guidance (QCA,* 2000a) and subsequently *The Early Years Foundation Stage* (DfES 2007)

Excellence and Enjoyment: A Strategy for Primary Schools (DfES, 2003b) is the document for *The Primary National Strategy*, combining the NLS and NNS, and stresses children's speaking and listening skills, as part of the drive for creativity to raise standards. However, it is debatable whether the majority of teachers ever have time to become familiar with and implement all the new initiatives and materials. This inability to keep up with initiatives and lack of attention to speaking and listening may become evident in my research.

Since this research project was undertaken, the *Primary Framework for literacy and mathematics* (DfES 2006) has potentially had time to have an impact in schools. This includes four strands dedicated to speaking and listening, which one would hope has increased the profile and status of both oral communication and the amount of collaborative work undertaken by children. It would be interesting to repeat this research project to determine whether or not this has improved attitudes to speaking and listening or increased collaborative teaching strategies.

This study is important to my current role as a teacher educator, as it may be able to highlight key training issues. These issues may either be absent or perhaps underemphasised in the initial teacher training curriculum. Chapter two sets the context by looking at research and theories, while chapter three explains my data collection methods. The findings are split into two chapters. Chapter four analyses pupil and teacher attitudes then chapter five examines discourse analysis. Finally, chapter six contains my reflections, conclusions and recommendations.

Chapter Two: Literature Review and Context for Research

This literature review draws on research and writing relating to peer talk and collaborative learning, including paired and group work; the relationship between talking, thinking and learning; the development of the child and its language, including constructivism, culture, class and gender; government and education policy; teacher strategies and attitudes; classroom management, such as group work or scaffolding; and the interpretation of language in classroom discussions, such as talk types and discourse analysis.

Learning Theories and Strategies.
This section considers a range of strategies that support learning, illustrated by several researchers, covering the following ideas:

- constructing knowledge through prior experience and active learning;
- interaction and learning through quality or exploratory talk;
- scaffolding: learning through adult intervention or peer support;
- peer collaboration: paired or group work;
- how talking, thinking and learning are interdependent.

A number of researchers have examined the importance of prior experience in affecting learning: experiential learning and constructivism. Piaget believes 'the process of learning involves active construction' and learning through active experiences (Stewart, 2004, p9). Dewey recognises the importance of active learning, stressing the significance of students' past experiences in affecting the way they learn. (Stewart, 2004, p9). Lillis and McKinney (2003, p.89) explain Bruner's argument: 'it is through interaction with others, especially through speech, that we construct and make sense of our world.' This idea of learners constructing their own knowledge is highlighted by Vygotsky and means that 'learners cannot be simply 'given' information or new ideas, but must do active mental work in order to understand them' (Fox, 2005, p.284).

Vygostsky differed from Piaget and Bruner in that his main concern was with the relationship between thought and language.' (Fontana 1992, p.53). Cohen and Lawrence support the view that 'Talk... occupies a crucial position in the classroom in any consideration of principal agents of learning.' (Cohen and Manion, 1989, p.129). It is clearly important, then, that talk should have a high priority in the school curriculum, to support children's learning and thinking skills. In addition, all the other subjects in the

7

curriculum are taught through the medium or spoken and written English, so talk enhances learning in all subjects.

Mercer, Wegerif and Dawes (1999, p.109) claim that 'language is used as a cognitive, cultural and pedagogic tool.' This puts language beyond a simple means of communicating instructions. Bruner (1978), cited in Lillis and McKinney (2003, p.31) refers to the support that adults and more capable peers can offer as 'scaffolding'. This is where an 'expert' models how to do something and then works alongside the learner who has a try themselves, so that finally the learner can do the task independently.

This develops and reaffirms the work of Vygotsky (1978), cited in Lillis and McKinney (2003, p.31), who highlight the vital role of adult guidance, or that of more capable peers, in moving forward a child's learning. This difference in what a child can do independently and what they can do being scaffolded by an expert is called the ZPD (Zone of Proximal Development). The ZPD can be defined as the distance between the real level of development and the potential level of development which is possible with more knowledgeable others (MKO's).

Harmon (2002) examines how paired talk can support learners who are trying to utilise independent word learning strategies to improve reading. Peer support can enhance word learning, as the participants can engage in meaningful dialogues; maintain control of their own learning; and each can bring their own experience to the learning context. However, there is still an adult facilitator who can intervene and scaffold the process where necessary. It could be argued that all paired or peer work needs this type of scaffolding at the beginning of the process.

Palincsar and Brown (1985), in applying Vygotsky's theories about dialogue and scaffolding, suggest that if child and adult dialogue outside school is important for promoting learning, it ought to be effective in school as well. Furthermore, dialogue among students might enhance collaborative problem solving. They developed the concept of *reciprocal teaching,* whereby the teacher initially *models* or gives explicit demonstrations of a learning activity or skill. Having been shown a strategy, the responsibility for learning and using the strategy is passed to the students, who then assume responsibility for their own learning. The key factor teachers should be aware of is that the transfer of responsibility should be matched to the needs and ability of learners and this transfer should be gradual

(Brown and Palincsar, 1985). Mayer (2002, 2003) described reciprocal teaching as focusing not on what to learn, but rather how to learn. The students are apprentices within a cooperative learning group.

Norman (1992), cited in Corden (2000, p.82), emphasises the importance of the National Oracy Project, which 'highlighted the learning potential of peer group discussions which are reflective and hypothetical and where speech is tentative and exploratory.' This reaffirms the dual values of children learning through talk itself, but also the importance of peer collaboration. Lillis and McKinney (2003, p.31) synthesise Vygotsky's view that 'learning to talk is very much about learning to think.' Language, however, does not simply reflect thought but is also influenced by culture and society. The OU Handbook *Research Methods in Education* suggests that 'socio-cultural' theory or research

> represents an approach in which language is considered a 'cultural tool' for learning, and which each parental generation of a society uses to guide the cognitive and social development of its children.

> (2001, p240)

Rojas-Drummond (in Goodman, Lillis, Maybin and Mercer, 2003, p.36) develops Vygotsky's expert/apprentice model and Bruner's 'scaffolding' to support learning, researching the value of *guided participation*, citing Rogoff's work in 1991. This is important as the individual learns through interaction with others. However, Rogoff's *guided participation* also describes a certain type of learning where the child actively engages the help of all those in its social environment, to solve a problem. Mattos (in Goodman, Lillis, Maybin and Mercer, 2003, p.55) extends the notion of collaborative work by examining the work of Donato (1994), who shows how peers of similar ability can scaffold each other's work without an adult expert. Donato's study (learners of a second language working in co-operative tasks) showed that learning is 'internalised' from one participant scaffolding the other and through verbalising learning.

Language and Cultural Differences.
Learning language is subjective to culture, bias, prejudice and values. This is exemplified by Ivanicõ (2003), who argues that language is communication, which varies according to cultural differences, uses and contexts. Therefore, it is important that teachers take into account a child's personal, social, cultural, economic, ethnic and religious background.

Cotton (1995, p.20) warns that 'Culture may influence the way in which a trainer or a learner views a particular role' and that 'To a large extent we live up to the expectations of others…' Language is not learned in isolation from the culture in which the learner is brought up. Language is needed to express thoughts, but in using words to express thoughts, views can change. Thinking can develop by listening and talking to others.

A BBC *Horizon* programme (2003) explains how anthropologist, Henshilwood, discovers a deliberately created artefact in an African cave, dating c70,000 years ago (much earlier than previously thought possible). *Horizon* (2003) advocates that thinking is a defining trait of humankind and that thinking, language and art occurred simultaneously. The expression of symbolic thought, through art, implies the presence of language and society. Sapir (cited in Wyse and Jones 2001, p.124) suggests that, 'Language is a great force of socialisation, probably the greatest that exists.' Talk is what enables humans to think, learn, communicate and alter their environment.

Shattuck's book *The Forbidden Experiment,* (1981) outlines the story of Victor, the 'wild boy' of Aveyron, who was captured/rescued and subsequently taught by the physician Itard. Victor showed 'no awareness of himself as a human person related in any way to the people who had captured him. He could not speak and made only weird, meaningless cries.' (p.5). Hicks (1995, p.5) points out:

> his ambitious goal of educating a completely unsocialised and therefore speechless child attests to the importance placed upon language as a symbolic tool of society…viewed as a crucial link in explaining how children become fully functional members of a social world.

It would appear that previous experiences and culture (or lack of it) had affected Victor's ability to learn language. Czerniewska (1992, p.21) advocates the importance of talk and its role within society:

> While some societies still have not developed a written language, all have complex oral forms and, within any society with a written culture, speaking is the most frequent activity for virtually all individuals.

Talk has had longer than written language to influence the creation of societies, written language being relatively recent. The socio-cultural approach emphasises the importance of different *types* of talk in developing thinking.

Hicks (1995, p.3) stresses that language is a unit of social communication, and discourse is never neutral or value free. Discussing children's language on entry to school with various teachers and on considering Bernstein's theory of the elaborate and restricted code, it becomes apparent that some children are struggling to access the school language and curriculum (Haralambos 1985, p.199). The theory suggests that working class children's restricted speech patterns put them at the disadvantage of not understanding the elaborate speech code of the classroom, unlike their middle-class peers. It suggests that to access the curriculum, these children would have to take on different beliefs and values which would conflict with their home values and personal identities.

This view is supported by Bourdieu, (cited in Bartlett, Burton and Peim 2001, p.186), who argues that a child's class can determine educational attainment. Children arrive at school with such different backgrounds, cultures and experiences, but some children can access the curriculum and classroom routine more easily because the language and culture of school is more like the language and culture of home. If children experience a big difference in home and school culture, it makes it more difficult for them to fit in the social norms of a middle-class education system. There is a conflict which can be resolved by either taking on and learning the new school culture and leaving it behind at the end of the school day, or by rebelling against the predominant school culture, for fear of losing their own identity or denying the home culture.

Hicks (1995, p.14) examines Heath's Study (1982, 1983) of the differences between black and white working class children's language patterns. The former group exhibit rich oral language traditions while the latter have limited vocabulary and short sentences, sticking to facts and not elaborating. This suggests that it is not simply an issue of class, as black and white working class language patterns vary. But again, this indicates how language ability makes access to the curriculum more difficult for children with limited language and vocabulary.

Torrance and Pryor's work (1998) shows the ambiguous nature of language and how easy it is to misinterpret what is said. They conclude 'Such ambiguous encounters are likely to carry consequences for individual children's learning.' (Torrance and Pryor 1998, p.32). This shows how language can have a multitude of meanings dependent on both speaker and listener's interpretation, showing that talk is interdependent with thinking and linked to the learner's prior experience and culture.

Alexander (2000, p.39) explores the discourse between teachers and students in different countries, asking what can be learned from this about cultural or national identity. It shows a vastly different way of questioning children and diverse expectations of how they should answer. Alexander does not confine himself to just observing literacy lessons to examine the role of talk. One example shows a mathematics lesson where Russian children are expected to give thorough and detailed explanations of their calculation methods. Consideration needs to be given whether different people learn in different ways because of their culture, or whether it is the culture that dictates the ways of learning. Galton (QCA, 2003c) refers to Alexander's international comparisons of pedagogy across different cultures and concludes 'it should not be assumed that teaching strategies that are effective in one country will always be equally effective in another.' (Galton: paper in QCA, 2003c, p.51).

Cultural transmission tends not to be that simple, but it seems the Russian model of teaching and learning promotes exploratory talk, problem solving skills and the ability to think more clearly. These traits are also apparent in Rojas-Drummond's analysis of Rogoff's work on High/Scope and cooperative learning in Mexican classrooms and Mercer's U.K. 'Talk Project' model, all of which contrast with the Indian 'transmission' model of learning, where the language exchanges are limited to initiation and response, rather than elaboration of questions and answers. According to Alexander (2000), in Russia there is feedback, in the form of encouragement and further questioning, which extends thinking and verbalises the process of problem solving. He aims to find out from what pattern of exchange pupils learn more and how to enhance the learning potential of classroom talk (Alexander in QCA, 2003c, pp.34-35). He concludes that dialogic teaching (use of language to move learning forward or learning and creating through dialogue) needs to be *collective:* teachers and pupils address learning tasks together (whole class or group).

Early Language Development and the Role of Parents.
Having considered the influence of culture on language acquisition and the place of language in different societies, the importance of early language development will be reviewed along with its impact on schooling. It is the low levels of linguistic ability that

concern many teachers in nursery and receptions classes. According to McClelland (2002):

> Anecdotal evidence, supported by a recent Trust survey of headteachers, suggests that more children are arriving into nursery education at three without the language skills appropriate for their age; vocabulary is less well developed than five years ago and there is a reduced capacity to listen.

There are many theories why this is the case, from working parents to the high number of hours children spend in front of the television. Whatever the reasons, it is accepted that a child's early linguistic experiences are crucial both to language development but also to the overall capacity to learn. The *Talk To Your Baby* is a campaign run by the National Literacy Trust (2005) and aims:

> to encourage parents and carers to talk more to children from birth to three. Talking to young children helps them become good communicators, which is essential if they are to do well at school and lead happy, fulfilled and successful lives.

There have been television adverts encouraging parents to talk to their children and leaflets and posters in health centres sending out this message. Another theme the *National Literacy Trust* is considering is whether children's buggies face the wrong way, preventing the face to face communication that was typical with old fashioned prams. *Sure Start* (2005) explains its mission as being 'the government programme to deliver the best start in life for every child. We bring together, early education, childcare, health and family support.' Other initiatives also encourage communication between parents and children. One of the aims of *Every Child Matters* (DfES, 2003a) is 'engaging and helping parents in actively supporting their children's learning and development.' Clearly, the importance of parents in their child's education and good links between home and school is at the forefront both politically and educationally. Again, communication and interaction are stressed.

Prior to schooling, children's linguistic development is supported by parents/carers, siblings, family and friends. The role of parents is usually the most significant factor in early communication skills. Hohmann (2005) discusses research and studies in America about early language development and the role of parents. She concludes the more parents talk to children, the more the children are able to talk. Hohmann (2005) confirms that higher pre-school spoken vocabulary levels can predict later reading success. She stresses that linguistic development depends on language being directed to the child and not just in the background.

Ely, Gleason and McCabe (1996) examine the role of parents in encouraging gender specific speech patterns and they focus on a characteristic of narrative style associated with gender, 'females use far more reported speech than males do…Narratives are an important way of conveying one's interpretation of the world…(1996, p.7). It seems that these gender differences are transmitted from parent to child, (Ely et al., 1996, p.8); that parents are more affectionate with girls; and more specifically there is 'evidence that mothers speak to toddlers more than fathers do and that they speak to their daughters more than they do to their sons' (Ely, Gleason and McCabe 1996, p.11). This difference in the way language is addressed to girls and boys means that 'parents express and perpetuate specific cultural and gender-based standards.' (Ely et al., 1996, p.19). It is a matter of debate whether gender traits are a true reflection of sex differences or whether they are a social construct. This highlights the importance of parent-child communication and its impact on linguistic development.

Maybin (2003, p159) considers how children use 'different voices', (informal, teacher-like, adult, child, social, academic) and move between them ('intertextual referencing'). It is interesting to note how children take on the voices of others, such as the authoritative teacher 'voice' or the casual social 'dialogue', or the on-task doing their school-work 'voice'. Maybin (n.d. in QCA 2003c, p.43) also focuses on how children's conversations show the use of 'specific language practices to explore issues relating to gender and identity.' In any classroom dialogue, it is not only the words that are important in evaluating a situation, but what those words represent and signify for the speakers, the cultural significance of the utterances. The importance of gender, clearly, is not confined to early language development, as outlined above by (Ely et al., 1996), but is evident in later schooling. This highlights the importance of early language experiences. There is also a discussion of gender in a later section, as it examines teaching strategies, but with a focus on boys. It also considers socioeconomic factors and whether English is the first language.

Government Policies and Teaching Strategies.

Teaching strategies, such as shared (whole class) and guided (small group) work, originating from the National Literacy Strategy, emphasise the role of the teacher. It is the teacher that models how to do something and then provides a scaffold for the children. Very little credence seems to be given to children collaborating and learning from each other. Edwards (n.d. in QCA 2003c, 39) suggests that children tend to have little experience of listening to each other. He offers a reason as being that for teachers, 'An absence of untoward noise is still commonly taken as evidence of good classroom control. Opening out the interaction risks disorder.' Edwards (n.d. in QCA 2003c, 38). Therefore teachers tend to dominate conversation. It appears that the role of talk is still underestimated in schools, the emphasis being on reading and writing, confirmed by the QCA:

> In the decade or so since the English national curriculum was produced, there has been a firm emphasis on raising standards in reading and writing. [but]… there seems far less confidence about how to teach or plan for progression in speaking and listening.

QCA (2003c, p.3)

This is despite clear evidence suggesting that improved skills in discourse result in higher standards of thinking. Galton concludes that:

> teachers should master the principles that empirical research has shown promote higher-order thinking. These include using open-ended questions, allowing suitable waiting times between asking the questions and persuading pupils to respond, and encouraging pupils to explain or elaborate their answers.

(Galton: paper in QCA, 2003c, p.51)

Furthermore, many teachers are unaware of the impact of how different ways of talk can improve thinking. It is ironic that speaking and listening have been so undervalued, as they have been part of important conclusions and recommendations in various reports. This series of reports: Primary Hadow (1931), Plowden (1967), Bullock (1975), the 1987 Language in the National Curriculum (LINC) and The National Oracy Project (1987-91), all conclude that spoken language is central to learning; that education should involve activity and experience; and that drama, talk and story telling are crucial elements of learning (Wyse and Jones 2001). Grugeon, Hubbard, Smith and Dawes (2001, p.7) state:

> the importance of talk had been gradually emerging as fundamental to children's learning. It was often acknowledged implicitly but rarely made explicit in planning for the majority of curriculum subjects.

There is a distinct lack of focus on talk, exacerbated by the fact that SATs, exams and tests are done individually, which means that collaborative work is undervalued. Wyse and Jones (2001, p.189) stress the importance of social interaction to promote language development. This improved language development leads to higher levels of thinking and learning. Cameron (n.d. in QCA 2003c, p65) cites the 1988 Kingman Report, which played a key role in shaping the National Curriculum, 'talk is not merely social and communicative, it is also a tool for learning.' This provides a rationale for focusing on oracy in education (p.66) but also examines the role of the teacher in promoting literacy and language in school. Cameron suggests teachers are often not facilitating 'learning through talk, because they are not supported adequately with the curriculum'. Cameron (n.d. in QCA 2003c, p72). Perhaps lack of appropriate training is also an issue to consider.

The difference in children's talking and thinking skills is apparent in Mercer's TRAC Programme (Talk Reasoning and Computers) which 'was a specially designed scheme of work made up of teacher-led and collaborative activities.' (Mercer, Wegerif and Dawes, 1999, p.98) This research investigated children's problem solving ability, both in groups and as individuals. It was the teacher's effective use of scaffolding strategies, which enabled a different type of thinking, including recap/ reformulation/ elicitation/ exhortation; effective questioning techniques; quality discussion through exploratory talk; the setting of clear ground rules; drawing on shared knowledge (Mercer, 2000, p158). The programme empowered children to 'discuss issues in more depth and for longer, participate more fully' (Mercer, 2000, p151).

Wray and Lewis's model (2005) has been used to exemplify an effective teaching and learning strategy and was adopted by the NLS: d*emonstration, joint activity, supported activity* and *individual activity*. Group work is initially supported, before becoming 'teacher-less'. Thus *demonstration* corresponds to teachers modelling how to do an aspect of literacy in a *joint activity*. The *supported activity* would be where the children try out the skill the teacher recently demonstrated or modelled, but the teacher is still present to offer support or scaffold learning (whole class or group). At this point, the children would do an individual activity, where they aim to use the skills learned without any support.

It seems there are arguments for both the teacher as 'expert' scaffolding learning and the teacher initially fulfilling this role and then moving aside to allow peer collaboration and peer scaffolding. This second scenario, however, still has intervention by the teacher, where necessary, to scaffold learning. But there is a third scenario, whereby children have developed competencies from having had effective initial teacher input, but groups are now teacher-less, because they can manage themselves.

Black and Wiliam (1998) examine effective methods of formative assessment: not only teachers giving targeted comments to enhance learning, but also including children giving each other feedback. Clearly, for this to work there needs to be thoughtful reflection, thinking in pairs and a commitment to all taking part in the process. The teacher needs to make pertinent observations that praise achievement, but also offer constructive comments for development. It involves extending and developing children's thinking, facilitating probing and speculation, and relies on effective classroom talk and interaction. (Alexander in QCA, 2003c, p.35).

Godhino and Shrimpton (2002, p.2) examined primary-age children's small group discussions about literature and observed that 'boys consistently dominated the discussions' and that teachers also exerted control over the discussion process. Godhino and Shrimpton (2002, p.4) discovered that many children lacked social and cooperative skills but moreover were not clear what constituted an effective discussion. Certain factors exacerbated this and one teacher, Ambrose, showed awareness that 'the cultural backgrounds of his students impact on the discussion dynamics. He acknowledges the need to adjust his discussion strategies accordingly...' Godhino and Shrimpton (2002, p.6) Children with ESL (English as a second language) gave particularly short answers as did children from lower socioeconomic backgrounds. The teachers in the study understand that:

> language is central to learning. Moreover, they both value small-group contexts where children have opportunities to learn through sharing their knowledge, and using talk to mediate their learning. Importantly, these teachers are aware of meeting the individual needs of both boys and girls.
>
> (Godhino and Shrimpton 2002, p.7)

The important conclusion is that gender differences were less significant than socio-cultural factors and that it is quality teaching practices that enable more equal opportunities for learning.

The Organisation of Group Work.

A number of researchers have considered the issue of managing the practicalities of group work and the often negative attitude of teachers, or indeed children, towards this method of classroom organisation. Fox (2005) explains that some children, even with joint tasks, will opt out and copy the work of others, while others take the opportunity to socialise. He suggests that adults find it hard to work in groups of over four people, due to the need for sophisticated management and communication skills, and that a pair could be the optimum group. He stresses the importance of 'training' groups to work together productively.

Gibbs (1994, p.9) comments on team size: small teams of three to four work faster and are easier to manage but may lack expertise; large teams of six to eight can cover for missing or slack members, but need clear roles and can lack organisation. It is possible that teachers have tried and given up on group work, when it has failed. However, as with any new teaching and learning strategy, the technique needs practice and teachers needs to model and scaffold the process initially.

Blum-Kulka and Snow (2004, 2005) examine language development through peer interaction and how peer talk fosters children's co-construction of their social and cultural worlds. This links language, culture, learning and collaboration, showing their mutual interdependence. This highlights the opportunities teachers have to promote learning through talk and collaboration, while taking into account children's current levels of knowledge and linguistic ability.

It is possible that teachers have a negative attitude to collaborative work in general. An American study by Leonard and Leonard (2003, abstract) highlighted that:

> The institutionalization of collaborative working environments is widely considered to be critical to the creation and maintenance of schools as professional learning communities. Prevailing thought suggests that improved student performance may be fully realized only when teachers routinely function as teams and abandon their traditional norms of isolationism and individualism

Leonard and Leonard (2003) find that teachers are often unwilling to work collaboratively because they are more concerned with competing with each other; or that it takes more time and they were not receiving extra pay; feel threatened by the ideas of others; lack interest in colleagues' ideas; and have an attitude that colleagues were lazy, hence preferring to work alone.

In contrast to negative attitudes, an Australian study by Sullivan (2002, p2) examined how a teacher, Gemma, could foster effective collaborative skills. Enabling peer culture, as opposed to adult culture, was an important factor that enhanced student motivation and learning. Sullivan (2002, p.6) observed:

> There seemed to be a positive collaborative climate in the classroom and a sense of community cohesiveness. Gemma and the students communicated with respect for each other and showed concern for each other's welfare...When someone was speaking, those listening gave eye contact ...I rarely heard or saw Gemma or students put others down.

Gustafson and MacDonald (2004, p.338) analysed transcripts of children's talk during a parachute building and testing exercise. Talk was used for sharing observations and justifying decisions. Children were observed to both express doubts that their parachute would not work and to offer not only encouragement but also design advice (Gustafson and MacDonald (2004, p.343). This shows evidence of children scaffolding each other's work; peer support and mutual learning through effective talk. It is also interesting to note that:

> During the course of completing the tasks, children engaged in recounting amusing anecdotes from their lives and expressed doubts, concerns, and frustrations related to the design task.
>
> (Gustafson and MacDonald, 2004, p.342)

This is significant because both Gustafson and MacDonald's work and that of Sullivan's above, show that children can still complete tasks even though they may spend some time talking about issues not relating to the task itself.

Opportunities for Talk.

The following section shows the inter relationship between talk, interaction, prior experience, teacher:pupil attitudes and class organisation. An ESRC funded research project (2005), *Using Talk to Activate Learners' Knowledge*, researched how teachers use talk to promote learning. Part of the conclusion showed that: 'Teacher talk dominates whole class teaching and there is relatively little interactivity...There is very little talk initiated by the children at all.' Some group tasks were set but it was evident from dialogues transcribed, that children were not making best use of this opportunity; it seems this aspect of work had not been modelled.

Sinclair and Coulthard (1975, p.16) point out that in a classroom situation, the teacher always has the right to speak whereas the child needs permission, such as putting a hand up to be nominated. This restricts the opportunities a child has to speak and also implies that what the teacher says is more important. Corden (2000, p.131) confirms teachers tend to dominate classroom talk but also suggests their questioning techniques neither encourage exploratory activity nor foster pupil participation. Corden (2000, p.86) recommends that teachers need to discuss ground rules with students, to promote a shared understanding of group tasks. Grugeon, Hubbard, Smith and Dawes (2001, p.74) state that 'Children need to be able to explain their views, justify choices, methods and decisions' and 'understand and value talk as a strategy for learning.'. Gibbs and Habeshaw (1989, p.75), although referring to students in HE, stress that:

> there is much to be gained from working collaboratively with others...develop students' ability to work creatively with ideas, to develop their ability to think things through and to develop communication skills.

Teachers need to be supported to facilitate and value this process, (Cameron n.d. in QCA 2003c, p72) and not to be concerned about issues such as loss of control, discipline problems or noise. (Edwards n.d. in QCA 2003c, 38).

In a small-scale research project in a secondary school (Buckley 2003), both teachers and children seem to think that if children were talking they were not working; that only writing down was 'proper work'. Most children and some teachers did recognise benefits of working together to move learning forward and improve social skills. Most teachers feel collaborative work is pointless and disruptive. Some paired and group work shows peer scaffolding and evidence of improved learning taking place. There are no significant differences in gender in the quality of talk but there is a great deal of variation by subject. The talk observed varies in quality, much of it lacking focus, with children seeming to be unclear about the purpose of collaborative talk.

Jaques (2000) stresses the importance of experiential learning, based on Kolb (1984). Learning comes from being involved in an experience, then reflecting on that activity, being committed to the aims of the group and to feel valued as part of the decision making and learning process. Wray and Lewis (2005) suggest that modern learning theory gives greater recognition to the importance of social interaction and that learners are social constructors of knowledge.

In collaboration with others, learners establish:

- shared consciousness: - a group working together can construct knowledge to a higher level than can the individuals in that group each working separately...
- borrowed consciousness: - individuals working alongside more knowledgeable others can 'borrow' their understanding of tasks and ideas to enable them to work successfully.

Learning, therefore, is dependent on one's ability to use language, mainly spoken, in order to share and reconstruct knowledge and experience. Hall (2005) claims that 'Neuroscience is confirming earlier psychological theories about the importance of emotional engagement in learning'. According to Cotton (1995): 'The deep learning approach turns other people's ideas into your own structure of knowledge.' It is a process of the active transformation of knowledge; requiring study and understanding; time; effort; and internal reflection. (Cotton 1995, p70.)

Blum-Kulka and Huck-Taglicht (2004) stress the importance of peer talk and how it 'offers children ample opportunities to listen in, practice and display conversational as well as academic discursive skills...' Dawes and Wegerif (1998) emphasise that talk needs explicit teaching; that children need to try out group exercises requiring joint decisions.

Talk Types and Discourse Analysis.
Finally the field of discourse analysis will be examined. Hicks (1995, p.3) explains the meaning of discourse as 'a dialectic of both linguistic form and social communicative practices.' and as 'oral and written texts that can be examined after the fact...' She further explains this by discussing 'Bakhtin (1981, 1986) [who] developed a theory of language centered around dialogic *utterances* as opposed to grammatical sentences...' Hicks (1995, p.3). Words have more than their dictionary meaning; they acquire meanings through social usage. Mercer (in QCA 2003c) defines another important concept in discourse analysis: that of *dialogic talk*. This is when 'both teachers and pupils make substantial and significant contributions and through which pupils' thinking on a given idea or theme is helped to move forward.' (Mercer n.d. in QCA 2003c, p.74)

Francis and Hunston (1998) explain that there is a need to define analytical categories to apply to discourse analysis. One issue is that it is difficult to ascertain how utterances are linked to previous or subsequent utterances. Another is their claim that 'only video recording can capture all the features of conversation' Francis and Hunston (1998, p.124). For ethical reasons, explained in the methodology, children's talk and interactions will be taped rather than videoed. Therefore, gesture, eye contact and intonation will not be clear from the conversation transcripts. The reader will need to rely on the researcher's interpretation of the transcripts as being informed by field observation and research notes.

Sinclair and Coulthard (1975, p.1) explain that the structure of classroom interactions are not straightforward to analyse; that discourse analysis can focus on grammar or structure; and that it is easy to mix up pedagogic structures with linguistic structures. By this they mean that language is classified by grammar and structure i.e. the position of subject and verb will indicate the type of utterance: declarative; interrogative; imperative; and the type of interaction: informative; elicitation; directive (Sinclair and Coulthard 1975, p.13). They confirm the issue highlighted by Francis and Hunston; that in real life situations there is a need to use information about the non-linguistic environment. This means that transcription needs to address more than what is spoken, as discourse analysis requires a fuller picture of how people communicate.

Another way of analysing utterances is to use Mercer's categories of talk. He analyses talk in terms of 'disputational', 'cumulative' and 'exploratory' utterances. Disputational talk tends to be 'a defensive, uncooperative encounter, in which the perspectives of the two participants compete with rather than complement each other' (Mercer, 2000, p.97). This leads to work tasks not being completed, or students not fulfilling their potential. Cumulative talk, in contrast, contains no argument but rather cooperation, with one speaker confirming the contribution and information of another. The speakers are uncritical of each other's contributions and although the work generally gets done there is a lack of development of new thinking (Mercer, 2000, p.31). Exploratory talk involves speakers accounting for their own opinions and challenging those of others in a constructive way. It often contains words such as, 'because', 'if', 'why' and 'I think' (Mercer, 2000, p.154).

Mercer, Wegerif and Dawes (1999, p.98) believe exploratory talk 'represents an 'educated' way of using language to construct knowledge which one would expect to be fostered by school experience.' (Mercer 2000). This level of analysis would give data on the

22

effectiveness of child-to-child talk in moving learning forward. There are also more specific options, such as 'concordancer' software packages (Mercer, Wegerif and Dawes1999) to log the frequency of certain words that show a higher order of discussion skills. These options will be discussed in the methodology.

This study will identify opportunities for children to talk to each other when doing work tasks and evaluate the quality of interactions. Ideally, tasks would be general, not just literacy based, but it would be unfeasible to do observations in all subjects. One factor to consider is the number of children in a group and how numbers may affect productivity, cooperation and task completion. The issue is that children are seated in groups by the teacher, but those teachers still ask them to work individually (Fox 2005, p.161). This was evident from making multiple observations as a Literacy Consultant, where very little genuine paired or group work was seen.

Summary:

Intrinsic to the thinking of those like Rogoff, Mercer and Alexander is a belief in the value of talk for learning… where pupils understand underlying principles and generalisations rather than merely grasping superficial understandings of specific experiences. In this way talk can be used to promote learning, rather than merely being used to parrot or mirror what the teacher has said. (Myhill, 2005)

To conclude, the initial objectives will be outlined and related to relevant readings. When identifying opportunities pupils have to work collaboratively through talk, it will be interesting to consider the work of: Jaques (2000), Gibbs and Habeshaw (1989), Mercer (2000), and Gibbs (1994). They all consider how learners operate in groups, including the influence of group size. When analysing types and quality of talk, it will be important to refer to the work on discourse analysis and language interpretation, by researchers such as: Mercer, Wegerif and Dawes (1999), Mercer (2000), Hicks (1995), Sinclair and Coulthard (1975), Francis and Hunstan (1998), Torrance and Pryor (1998), Gustafson and Macdonald (2004). There are various speech types or utterances, plus different ways of analysing them. It seems that it is more than the words themselves that convey meaning.

Examining exchanges between children should offer an insight on whether paired or group talk supports or hinders task completion, and may suggest reasons why. Looking for evidence of pupils scaffolding each other's learning links to work by: Palinscar and Brown (1985), Harmon (2002), Rojas-Drummond (2000) and Mattos (2000), who outline how either an adult expert or more knowledgeable peer can move learning on. It is important to determine teachers' attitudes to collaborative work, whether negative: Leonard and Leonard (2003); or positive; Sullivan (2002), as this will be a major factor whether peer group work is successful, or whether such interaction takes place.

There are other issues that have arisen while reviewing the literature. Important consideration needs to be given to the role of prior experience and linguistic development, which affect how children learn: Fox (2005), Stewart (2004), Lillis and McKinney (2003), Wray and Lewis, Cotton (1995). There is also the role of culture, including gender and class: Ivanicō (2003), Godhino and Shrimpton, Maybin and Alexander (2000). Factors such as social background need keeping in mind when considering the overall aim of investigating the relationship between peer talk, collaborative work and learning. There is also the role of government and educational policy to consider: Wyse and Jones (2001), Grugeon et al (2001) and Cameron, (2003). These policies and initiatives play an important role in determining the rationale and priorities of the curriculum.

Having highlighted which writers research relate to the different objectives of this study, this section concludes by examining whether there are any conflicts between researchers or any differences in emphasis. It is interesting to note that the research relevant to this study is not contradictory; the differences relate to matters of emphasis. The focus for researchers such as Jaques (2000), Gibbs and Habeshaw (1989), Mercer (2000), and Gibbs (1994), is the interaction between group members and the roles individuals play within groups of different sizes. The work of Mercer, Wegerif and Dawes (1999), Mercer (2000), Hicks (1995), Sinclair and Coulthard (1975), Francis and Hunstan (1998), Torrance and Pryor (1998), Gustafson and Macdonald (2004), focus more on the quality of talk during group work and how the use of words can be interpreted.

Fox (2005), Stewart (2004), Lillis and McKinney (2003), Wray and Lewis, Cotton (1995) would be more concerned with how language is learned and developed, teaching strategies and how children acquire new knowledge. This has an influence on how children operate within groups and the types and quality of talk exhibited. Palinscar and Brown (1985), Harmon (2002), Rojas-Drummond (2000) and Mattos (2000) highlight the role of scaffolding and guidance, to enhance language and learning. The level of language developed will then have an influence on how successfully children collaborate in paired or group work.

Writers such as Ivanicō (2003), Godhino and Shrimpton, Maybin and Alexander (2000) see culture as the driving force behind children's learning. Gender, class and the values of the society children live in has an impact of how children develop language and how this language may be utilised to promote effective learning. This learning may further be influenced by scaffolding by experts or peer group work. Teachers' attitudes to collaborative work is seen as important by Leonard and Leonard (2003) and Sullivan (2002), as this tends to control how many opportunities children have to work collaboratively. It is the role of government and educational policy that writers such as Wyse and Jones (2001), Grugeon et al (2001) and Cameron, (2003), consider as critical. This includes how the curriculum affects the learning and teaching of oracy; which teaching strategies are employed; and the relative importance attributed to oral skills and collaborative work. This study should draw on a range of these ideas.

Chapter Three: Methodology and Research Activity

Theoretical Location of the Work.

The purpose of the methodology is to consider the best way of fulfilling the aim of this research project. A review of research has highlighted several related studies and areas to consider: different methods of discourse analysis; the impact of classroom management on collaborative work; features of paired and group work; types of talk; other classroom observations relating to talk; and learning theory. This methodology should inform the choice of appropriate data collection methods to meet the objectives of the research.

Objectives ~ *Research Method*

- To identify the opportunities that pupils have to work collaboratively through talk ~ *Observation notes and recording of child-to-child talk and interaction.*

- To analyse the types and quality of talk ~ *Analysis of recorded dialogues of child-to-child talk and interaction.*

- To investigate whether opportunities for paired or group talk support or hinder task completion ~ *Observation notes, recording of child-to-child talk and interaction, examination of work produced by children.*

- To look for evidence of pupils scaffolding each other's learning ~ *Observation, recording and analysis of child-to-child talk and interaction.*

- To explore pupils' and teachers' attitudes to paired and group talk ~ *Mainly in interviews and questionnaires. Partly through observation notes and recording of child to child talk and interaction.*

Selection of School

I originally considered using three contrasting schools and selecting one year group to compare data between (provisionally Y4). On reflection, only one school was used as a case study, as my original idea would have provided too much data for this size of research project. Therefore, I approached the Head of a school I worked with as a Literacy Consultant. They were happy to take part because speaking and listening were a priority. It could be argued that my research may not show a typical portrait of the amount of collaborative work going on in Primary Schools. However, the Head felt they were at the beginning of a process of increasing speaking and listening. It is possible, however, that there may be an atypically high proportion of positive attitudes towards collaborative work.

Overview of research methodology

(A full research timetable can be viewed in appendix C1 p.96).

My study involved observation of pupils in literacy lessons; transcribing and analysing children's dialogues; distributing staff and children's questionnaires; and recording interviews with a number of staff and with groups of children.

Methodology	
Data sample:	One primary school.
Number of classes:	Eight, including Two Nursery Classes (am/pm class).
Teachers:	Ten – including Head and part-time SEN Teacher.
Questionnaires:	8 teachers and 7 support staff completed the forms. (The ten planned originally included Head Teacher and part-time Special Needs Teacher. The Head preferred class teachers to answer questionnaires, as this was more representative of daily teaching routines) 166 children completed forms, from all 8 classes.
Interviews:	Four teachers: a representative from each of Foundation; KS1; Lower KS2; Upper KS2 (to include the Literacy Co-ordinator).
Group interviews:	Children's groups finally involved 4 from each class (2 boys and 2 girls) and these fours were grouped in eights. Foundation (Nursery/Reception); KS1 (Y1/Y2); Lower KS2 (Y3/Y4); Upper KS2 (Y5/Y6). This enabled all classes to be represented.
Number of lessons observed:	One literacy lesson was observed in each class (7 in total – only one nursery class was observed, so each year was seen once).
Number of dialogues recorded:	Seven lessons were observed, which included 22 taped dialogues (pairs and groups, duration 1 to 20 mins)

Research Methodology

According to Cohen, Manion & Morrison (2000, p.3), 'Research is concerned with understanding the world and that this is informed by how we view our world(s).' Research can also be viewed as 'the selection and analysis of data with a view to the provision of valid and useful information' (OU Handbook, 2001, p.10). This implies research has a purpose to inform policy making or to improve practice. My review of the literature shows how important and current the focus of my research is and how its findings could directly improve professional practice.

Many practitioners in the field of education and social sciences view research as remote and academically difficult. Indeed for some, research seems unnecessary and irrelevant; undertaken by academics who are no longer practitioners. However, Denscombe (1998, p.1) points out, 'Social research is no longer the concern of the small elite of professionals and researchers'. Research, therefore, needs promoting as a useful tool to support and improve practice.

Traditionally, research has high status and its methodological features are empirically based and therefore based on facts and statistics rather than values and subjective observations. However, educational research can also strive to observe and understand people's behaviour and interactions, therefore statistical analysis alone would not be a sufficient research method. Bell (1998, p.8) suggests that some researchers 'doubt whether social "facts" exist and question whether a "scientific" approach can be used when dealing with human beings.' This is highly relevant, as this research will have children as its subject.

Characteristics often associated with the natural sciences include:

> The testing of claims against empirical evidence… The quantitative measurement of phenomena. Experimental or statistical manipulation of variables to test causal hypotheses. A focus on facts rather than values. A concern to maintain objectivity, to avoid bias due to personal preferences.

> (OU Handbook, 2001, p.10)

These characteristics are not easily applied to studying behaviour, so different criteria have been formulated for qualitative research. In qualitative research, 'The researcher's identity, values and beliefs can not be entirely eliminated from the process – again in stark contrast to the ambitions of a positivistic approach to social research.' (Denscombe 1998, p.208). Nevertheless, researchers can draw on a variety of qualitative and quantitative techniques. Cohen, Manion and Morrison (2000, p.248) illustrate the two research methodologies, when referring to questionnaires, stating:

> Where measurement is sought then a quantitative approach is required; where rich and personal data are sought, then a word-base qualitative approach might be more suitable.

According to Thomas Kuhn (1962, p.10), referring to scientific theories, a paradigm is when two characteristics apply: when a researcher's

> achievement was sufficiently unprecedented to attract an enduring group of adherents away from competing modes of scientific activity. Simultaneously, it was sufficiently open-ended to leave all sorts of problems for the redefined group of practitioners to resolve.

A paradigm, therefore, is a model or theoretical framework that can alter with new ideas and research. In terms of educational research there are at least two competing paradigms, each with their own supporters, although many researchers draw from both.

The Positivist theory uses quantitative methodologies; promotes objectivity and aims to look for patterns to explain behaviour. Critics argue human behaviour is not treated in a purely 'scientific' way, as people's actions are not necessarily measurable, repeatable, predictable or consistent. Conversely, the Interpretive paradigm uses qualitative methodologies; promotes subjectivity, in that the researcher's own views could impact on findings; aims to understand and interpret the individual's behaviour and actions; and requires the researcher to be an insider in the process, such as questioning research subjects while they are working/studying. This approach takes into account its subjects' own interpretations of the world. Critics argue this approach is open to the researcher's bias and prejudice, and by being an insider the researcher can influence the behaviour of subjects. (Cohen and Manion 1980).

It is important, therefore, for researchers' to question personal assumptions before selecting research methods. Another factor is whether the prejudices or motives behind the research will affect the validity of research findings, for example, school managers may want to research children's learning but have an underlying motive related to judging teachers' performance. This is highlighted by Denscombe (2002, p.177) who reinforces the need for ethics and researcher's integrity,

> because findings from research can have consequences – political, commercial, personal – that can invite the possibility of corruption... for instance, pressure from sponsors of research to produce findings that are not critical...

This introduces ethical dilemmas in research.

Ethical Considerations

Several ethical issues need considering in educational and social science research. If researching 'children's talk in the classroom' it is vital for the teacher to know they are neither being judged nor reported on. The Head assured staff confidentiality would be maintained and that research would help assess how far their efforts to promote speaking and listening had progressed. Staff were unanimous that my findings would be beneficial to their development and suggested repeating the research in the future to monitor their progress with collaborative work. All parties involved: school, teachers, children and parents 'will have to be convinced of your integrity and of the value of the research before they decide whether or not to cooperate.' Bell (1999, p.37). This would normally be a formal written approach to all concerned and if participation is agreed, written permission would be required from all participants. Certain procedures need adhering to, including confidentiality and anonymity of subjects; care and safety when research involves children; and that even if 'informed consent' is given, participants may still withdraw.

A staff consent form was sent to the school with a parental consent letter. The Head had a staff meeting to read my proposal; staff agreed verbally; and the Head signed consent on their behalf. She decided not to send my parental consent letter out, as from experience with other school letters, she anticipated a low rate of return. Consequently, she adapted it and used the school's headed paper, using 'negative response' for agreeing for children to take part. This was the procedure commonly used by the school, so the letter explained the research project and if parents objected, they should contact the school. Fortunately no parents objected to their child taking part. The Head explained the research to the children in assembly and it was agreed that I would ask for the children's consent before the lesson (only one child objected, so was not part of this research study).

A researcher needs to clarify who will see the data and whether or not participants will have the opportunity to comment on it before the report is written. Staff were keen for early feedback, even though I explained my research project would not be completed for some months. The Head asked if I could provide a preliminary report before the end of term, so they had something to discuss. Many staff expressed an overview was sufficient but I explained they would also get a fuller final report. Staff had different ideas about the level of detail they would like to see in their final report, some wanted a brief overview but others were keen to read my review of literature and detailed analysis of dialogues.

Another issue to consider is how the researcher alters the behaviour of participants. Children may be more honest to an outsider than to their teacher; teachers may be more honest to an outsider rather than to the management team. Tilstone (1998, p.126-127) points out, 'Observation may well be regarded as *spying* and, consequently, tact, honesty and sensitivity are essential if such basic rights as dignity, respect and privacy are not violated.' For my previous research, *An investigation into the opportunities for peer group talk in the classroom*, (secondary pupils), I found the children did ask questions and talk to me, but I believe that it was because they felt at ease in my presence; they talked openly, as if I had not been there.

Questionnaires and Interviews

An important factor in planning interviews is not to cover all the same material that the questionnaire deals with, but it allows a more in-depth exploration of questions from the paper surveys. Cohen and Manion (1980, p.241) question the value of having a '*formal interview* in which set questions are asked and the answers recorded on a standardised schedule.' Consequently I prefer to use a semi-structured interview, where I have certain questions in mind, which can be modified and added to, depending upon the responses. Although interviewers can be prone to bias (using questions to support their pre-conceived ideas), the advantage is that greater depth can be explored.

Bell (1999, p.135) points out that:

> Analysing responses can present problems, and wording the questions is almost as demanding for interviews as it is for questionnaires... the interview can yield rich material and can often put flesh on the bones for questionnaire responses.

In a questionnaire, I would not use all open questions but a mixture. As Bell (1999, p.127-128) suggests, the questionnaire was 'piloted to test how long it takes recipients to complete them, to check that all answers and instructions are clear and to enable [me] to remove any items which do not yield useable data'. As anticipated, changes were made in the light of feedback given by four teachers who piloted the questionnaire. There were questions added offering more open-ended comments to be made. The two teachers who piloted the interviews felt that they were lasting too long, so the number of questions was reduced.

Questionnaires for Staff

I decided to use questionnaires (appendix B1 p90), as I would not be able to interview all staff. This would enable me to gather data from a greater number of individuals than interviewing alone. This method provides information on attitudes to collaborative work and practical aspects of managing the process. I was keen to include support staff in questionnaires, as their opinions were valuable and could also be compared with those of the teachers. As there are often problems with questionnaire returns, a deadline of one week was agreed. A folder was left in the staff-room so returns were confidential. Another problem could be people not answering truthfully. However, I am able to triangulate findings by cross-referencing answers on the questionnaire with classroom observations. Triangulation uses 'several methods to explore an issue' which 'greatly increases the chances of accuracy.' (OU Handbook, 2001, p.65)

Questionnaires for Children

I was keen to use questionnaires with children (appendix B2 p92) to gather a large amount of data, but wanted to make them child-friendly. I designed a simple proforma, only asking children to state how they preferred to work, giving them a choice of 3 answers: alone, in pairs or in groups. It also asked them to give reasons for their choice. This would enable me to collect data on children's attitudes to collaborative work. A system was organised where children who could not fill questionnaires themselves had help from the class teacher, support staff or me.

> To make the questionnaire easier for respondents, the questions vary. Some can be open-ended, requiring more time to answer; and others a response to a statement. This could either be by indicating a number, such as the Likert scale, where data can be analysed in statistical software packages, such as *SPSS;* or using dichotomous questions, requiring a 'yes'/'no' response.
>
> (McNiff, Lomax and Whitehead 1996, p)

However, this makes them hard to analyse and classify. In contrast, Cohen, Manion and Morrison (2000, p.249) advocate:

> Avoid too many open-ended questions on self-completion questionnaires… [because they] cannot probe respondents to find out just what they mean… moreover, are too demanding of most respondents' time.'

On the children's questionnaire, there was only one main question with a choice of three answers and a space to write the reason.

32

Interviews for Staff

Staff interviews (appendix B3 p93), were necessary to add to the information from questionnaires. Interviews would enable me to probe in more depth and allow issues to arise not covered on the questionnaire. Selection of interviewees was considered and I decided on representatives from across the class age range, as there would be different factors involved in peer collaboration, speaking and listening across the age groups. This was discussed at the staff meeting before the research began. The interview should be a representative from Foundation, KS1, Lower KS2 and Upper KS2. Staff agreed, but the issue arose of whether the interviewees could see the questions in advance. I had considered this, as my reading about research methodology had flagged up this issue. Bell (1999) proposed that questions could be given in advance, to 'brief' the interviewee and due to the time limits involved, which might put staff under pressure. Therefore, I thought I would get a fuller understanding of staff attitudes if they had chance to do some preparation. They agreed with this aspect, but also said they would feel less nervous if they knew the questions in advance.

I did ask if those interviewed could include the Literacy Co-ordinator, as her input as the specialist in school would be useful. I also enquired whether I should interview support staff (TAs -Teaching Assistants and Nursery Nurse), but the consensus was they would feel happier simply filling in questionnaires.

Interviews with Children

A key issue when interviewing is to put interviewees at ease, so I decided not to interview children individually, being aware how intimidating this could be. Small groups were interviewed to obtain a collective view and encourage wider participation. Selecting a sample for pupil groups entailed ensuring a balance of age and gender. (appendix B4 p95). I felt this would enhance the information gleaned from questionnaires. I originally planned to have 6 children from 4 classes covering a range of ages, but on discussion with staff it was decided to have representatives from each class and combine 2 year groups together. To balance gender it was agreed that 2 boys and 2 girls would be chosen from each year group: N with R; Y1/Y2; Y3/Y4; and Y5/Y6. I did express concerns that 8 was a large group, but it was felt that 4 (1 boy and 1 girl from each class, in paired year groups) would be too small, if some children decided not to speak much.

Observation

My main method of data collection was observation, which Simpson and Tuson (1995, p.3) point out, can be 'difficult and complex, but is also one of the most versatile ways of gathering information.' Observation enables a researcher to triangulate, or cross-check data from questionnaires and interviews. Denscombe (1998, p.139) cites the advantage of observation being that:

> It does not rely on what people *say* they do, or what they *say* they think... it draws on the direct evidence of the eye to witness events first hand... it is best to observe what actually happens.

The best approach is an unstructured framework, which 'has no predetermined categories, but records as much of what happened as is possible...' rather than a structured framework which will 'generate data which can be used for statistical analysis...' but is less comprehensive and flexible (Clark and Leat, cited in Tilstone 1998, p.75). I recorded children talking when collaborating on work, which can, according to Simpson and Tuson (1995, p.53) 'take an inordinate amount of time to transform into transcripts... [but are] an invaluable tool... in the detailed study of pupils' talk.' I logged, using a schedule, the number of minutes in a lesson where children worked in pairs or groups; and kept a reflective research diary.

Observation and Field Notes

Observation and open-ended research field notes were vital in obtaining necessary data. I decided on an informal ring-bound book, so I could note details of children's names (they selected their own made-up name), and allocated them a number on a seating plan, to help later transcription. I was also keen to jot notes of children's behaviour and actions, but this was hard to do in addition to needing to write some of what they said, (which would facilitate transcribing). Clearly, videoing would be easier. Notes were also be made on matters such as whether the teacher gave explicit permission for children to work collaboratively; whether children tended to favour pairs or groups; how much time in lessons children were able to talk to each other; whether collaborative talk was in whole class or group work time; whether tasks set by the teacher were completed.

Unlike my research in a secondary school setting, the primary school observations were of different classes of children. This enabled me to determine how larger samples of children interacted. It was also necessary in order to observe different class teachers, to ensure

34

that data is not skewed by one teaching style (one teacher may always/never use paired talk). I originally planned to do 3 lesson observations per class, but this could have provided too much data for this size of research project. It was decided to do one observation of each class and consideration was given whether to observe a variety of subjects or keep to the same lesson in each. It seemed that observing the same lesson would offer a fairer comparison between classes and that the subject should be literacy, being my professional specialism. Also, literacy was the area in which the school was most interested in assessing their progress.

The difficulty with observations can be, as Bell (1999, p.157) suggests, 'The observers will have their own particular focus and interpret significant events in their own way.' Two observers of the same event could record differences in their findings due to subjectivity. It may be better to be a non-participant observer; not joining in activities, but simply recording aspects of behaviour i.e. children talking to each other. The weakness of this approach is that other interesting research data may be overlooked. The advantage should be reduced bias, as participant observers can become too immersed into the group being observed, which can lead to lack of focus. However, it would be very difficult in primary classrooms to remain aloof and would be rude to deliberately not speak to children, to fulfil a fully non-participant observer role. Cohen, Manion and Morrison (2000, p.187) quote King (1979) who avoided participant status:

> I kept standing so that physical height created social distance... did not show immediate interest in what the children were doing, or talk to them... avoided eye contact...

My aim was a compromise of getting children to feel comfortable with my presence but without skewing the research findings by over-familiarity. In reality, a researcher is neither participant nor non-participant observer, but somewhere on a continuum.

Recording and Transcribing Talk

I had originally considered videoing children working, as it would have been easy to see which child was talking, which would have helped the transcription process. Coulthard (2002) highlights that the police record interviews. Although many are tape-recorded, others use video, in order to show exactly what took place. This is because transcribed interviews cannot easily show a full picture of what actually happens, as intonation and non-verbal clues are needed for full meaning. However with video, ethically speaking, children in the study would no longer be anonymous. It could also have been more distracting or intrusive for the children, who may have either played up to a camera more so than with a tape recorder, or been inhibited by it. The school was reluctant to use video and suggested that more parents might object to video than to tape-recording. It was decided to use a MiniDisc recorder, as this was small, portable and could hold more data than a cassette.

A colleague, researching children's talk in mathematics, suggested certain equipment to request from the technician and specific practical methods to achieve better results. Microphones pick up sounds from different directions, so it was vital to ensure that minimal background noise was recorded. He gave me a copy of Jeffersonian Transcription Notation. (Jefferson (1984) cited in Atkinson and Heritage (eds.) (1984)). I used this when transcribing child to child dialogues.

Analysing Talk

Sinclair (2002, p.79) suggests 'the conventional meaning of an utterance was but a stage in its interpretation' highlighting that the same words have different meanings depending on the way they are said: intonation and body language. Therefore, field observation notes were used in conjunction with transcribed dialogues, where there was any ambiguity about meaning. I used Mercer's categories of disputational, cumulative and exploratory talk, as outlined in the literature review (Mercer 2000). This level of analysis would give data on the types and quality of talk; indicate how opportunities for paired or group talk affected task completion; and highlight any evidence of pupils scaffolding each other's learning. I had considered some other options, such as 'concordancer' software packages (Mercer, Wegerif and Dawes1999). These log the frequency of certain words, such as because/agree/I think, which show a higher order of discussion skills. However, I felt that this was probably unnecessary in such a small-scale study, and I did not have access to this technology.

Summary

To conclude, the researcher has to have a clear focus about what they are trying to find out and to select appropriate methods to obtain the required data. The choice of research methods varies according to the assumptions of researchers and the types of data needed. Much research in Education uses more qualitative data, such as observations and interviews, rather than quantitative, statistical data. There are inherent weaknesses in all methodologies, but as long as the researcher is aware of these, it is possible to minimise them. Also, by using a variety of methods it is possible to triangulate or cross-check the findings. It is important to address ethical issues while conducting research, to protect the subjects of the study and to give them enough information to obtain their informed consent. Research subjects need to understand the value of the intended research, perhaps how it might improve practice, and feel valued for their participation. Questionnaires, interviews and observations need to be sensitive of participants and focussed to meet the aims of the research. I used a combination of observation, discourse analysis, questionnaires and interviews to collect and triangulate my data. I will be reviewing the effectiveness of the research process later in this study, both in relation to reporting on specific data and in an overview in the concluding section.

Chapter Four: Findings and Discussion of Results
~ Pupil and Teacher Data

My research aim was to investigate the relationship between peer talk, collaborative work and learning. I intend to present my findings by examining data for each research objective. I will begin by examining the final objective: pupil and teacher attitudes towards paired and group talk, using data from field notes, teacher and pupil questionnaires and interviews. Findings from the discourse analysis and the other research objectives will be in a separate chapter. This table shows the actual duration of collaborative work time that occurred in each lesson observed and the number of times it occurred.

Opportunities for Collaborative Talk			
Class	Task	Number of minutes	Number of Children
N	1	20 minutes	Group of 6
R	1	20 minutes	Group of 5
Y1	1	10 minutes	Pair
	2	2 minutes	Pair
	3	2 minutes	Pair
	4	20 minutes	Group of 6
Y2	1	1 minute	Pair
	2	5 minutes	Pair
	3	Less than 1 minute	Pair
	4	15 minutes	Group of 4
Y3	1	2 minutes	Pair
	2	2 minutes	Pair
	3	3 minutes	Pair
	4	20 minutes	Group of 4
Y4	1	1 minute	Pair
	2	1 minute	Pair
	3	1 minute	Pair
	4	15 minutes	Group of 4
Y5	1	5 minutes	Group of 4
	2	15 minutes	Group of 5
	3	10 minutes	Group of 3
Y6	1	15 minutes	Group of 5
TOTALS	22 tasks	Average 23 mins	Pairs: 12	Groups: 10

In eight lessons, lasting approximately one hour each, there was a total of 186 minutes (3 hours and 6 minutes) of collaborative work. However, the actual teaching time often varied between 45 minutes to and one hour 10, allowing for children to enter, settle, clear up and leave. Therefore it would be difficult to calculate an accurate percentage of collaborative work- time, as opposed to teacher-led work time, as the length of a lesson varies.

Every lesson contained between 15 and 34 minutes of collaborative work: an average of 23 minutes per class. Although there were slightly more paired activities than group ones, paired work only totalled 31 minutes whereas group work lasted155 minutes. This could imply that either teachers value group work more or find it easier to manage. Nursery, Reception, Y5 and Y6 were all group work activities, whereas the other year groups had a combination of paired and group work.

The group tasks were nearly always long ones (15-20 minutes) and most paired work lasted 1 or 2 minutes. Year 6 did the least amount of collaborative work, with most being done by Y1 and Y5, but arguably the Y6 work was highly effective. Most collaboration in pairs was done before the children went to work at their tables, but most group work was done after the teacher input session, where children sat back at their tables.

Pupil Attitude ~ Children's Questionnaires

How do you prefer to work in class, most of the time?						
Year Group	On my own		In a pair		In a group	
Nursery (19)	5	26%	6	32%	8	42%
Reception (20)	5	25%	9	45%	6	30%
Year 1 (23)	4	17%	10	44%	9	39%
Year 2 (19)	6	32%	7	36%	6	32%
Year 3 (23)	10	44%	13	56%	0	0%
Year 4 (21)	7	33%	5	24%	9	43%
Year 5 (19)	1	5%	14	74%	4	21%
Year 6 (22)	2	9%	12	55%	8	36%
Total (166)	40	24%	76	46%	50	30%

The questionnaires show the majority of children (76%) favour paired or group work (46% and 30% respectively). However, a significant minority (24%) expressed a preference for working on their own. The table below shows the reasons for the choice of working preference.

How do you prefer to work in class, most of the time?		
Whole school	**166 responses**	

* Please note, the child may have given more than one reason for their preference, or none at all, therefore the tally for reasons may differ from the total number given for preferred way of working.

Reasons expressed for preference.		
I prefer to work on my own	**24%**	**40***
• I don't like people copying me/don't like giving them answers.		2
• I like working on my own/I get more work done on my own.		8
• I don't need any help.		2
• Because I think of good ideas myself.		4
• Quieter/no one to talk to or distract me/concentrate more.		11
• I prefer to sit on my own/I don't like people leaning on me.		2
• To get work done faster.		7
• I learn more on my own/I learn from my mistakes.		2
• I like working by myself because people work in different ways.		1
• To do more of my work without being annoyed by other people/in a group everyone shouts/people fall out in groups.		5
• So I don't copy.		1
I prefer to work in a pair	**46%**	**76***
• Friend can help/tell me what to do/I get stuck and need help.		18
• It's fun.		2
• In a group everybody takes your answers.		2
• In a group, there is too much noise and talking/no one distracts us in a pair/groups are too crowded, quite hard to ask for help.		9
• In a group half of them switch off.		1
• Because in a pair we can help each other/discuss our answers/share our ideas/talk about your answer/get more work and more answers.		24
• Easier to work with someone you know/can sit with your best friend/prefer to work with a friend/do not like working on own.		19
• It's easier than in a group or on your own/too hard if on own.		5
• With one friend it is quieter/you can concentrate/work faster.		7
• In a group you fight/argue/disagree/have too many opinions.		6
I prefer to work in a group	**30%**	**50***
• Because you can discuss your answers/help each other/share ideas/ questions/talk about work/exchange answers/more ideas your head.		27
• I like to work with my friends.		5
• So others can help me/give me ideas/tell me the answer.		6
• I prefer to work with others in a group.		3
• You work better.		1
• Because it's easier.		2
• It's fun.		1
• Working together helps you to get along and listen to other people.		1

Summary of Reasons for Preference.

Comments on working preferences provide a useful insight into children's attitudes to learning.

On my own:
- To avoid distraction, enhancing concentration.
- To get more work done, completing it faster.
- To use own ideas, avoiding others copying work.
- To work without help, learning from own mistakes.

In a pair:
- To work collaboratively, by sharing ideas and discussing answers.
- To work with a friend, giving more confidence and making it easier to complete the work.
- To avoid the disruptive elements of group work, such as noise and arguments.
- To prevent the situation that can arise in a group, where others take answers without doing any work.
- This confirms the view of Fox (2005), who suggests that a pair could be the optimum group for productivity and equality of workload.

In a group:
- To work collaboratively by sharing a wider range of ideas; exchanging, discussing, and then selecting answers.
- To get ideas or answers from others, without offering own suggestions.
- To work with friends, making the task easier and enjoyable.

It is possible to examine children's reasons by year group. I have included two contrasting groups; other data can be found in appendix E1 p158.

How do you prefer to work in class, most of the time?		
Year 3	23 responses	
* Please note, the child may have given more than one reason for their preference, or none at all, therefore the tally for reasons may differ from the total number given for preferred way of working.		
Reasons expressed for preference.		
I prefer to work on my own	44%	10*
• Because it's good when no one distracts me.		1
• I can work faster.		3
• Because I can be quiet.		1
• I don't like people copying me.		1
• I don't like people leaning on me.		1
• It's much better.		1
• I like to get my own work done/your friend doesn't ask you what to do.		2
I prefer to work in a pair	56%	13*
• I want to work with a friend because when I am stuck they can help me/the work is hard		3
• No one distracts us.		1
• Because he will help me and I will help him/I like sharing my ideas/help each other.		3
• Because we get on well with each other/because you get to work with your best mate.		5
• Because I can work with a friend - I don't like to be on my own.		1
• Because a group is more noisy.		1
• Because if you work in a group, half of them switch off.		1
I prefer to work in a group	0%	0*

Significantly, no children in Y3 chose to work in a group whereas in Y4, 43% selected group work as a preference. Looking at the responses of the Y3 class, many opted for paired or individual work because they felt group work was distracting and noisy. The majority (56%), who chose to work in pairs, stress the benefit of sharing ideas but also being able to work with friends. During the lesson observation, there were three paired tasks and one group task. The paired work was more productive than the group work, which both matches the children's attitudes (they favoured either working alone or pairs and were negative about group work) and it also reflects Fox's view (2005), that pairs could be the optimum grouping for effective learning.

How do you prefer to work in class, most of the time?		
Year 4	21 responses	
* Please note, the child may have given more than one reason for their preference, or none at all, therefore the tally for reasons may differ from the total number given for preferred way of working.		
Reasons expressed for preference.		
I prefer to work on my own	33%	7*
• Because in a group everyone shouts and it puts you off/is shouting at you when you try to say something.		2
• Because everyone gets me to talk and then I can't do it.		1
• I get more work done on my own.		2
• I can use my own ideas/get my own answers what I think.		2
• Because I end up moaning at people when they think they're right but I think they're wrong.		1
• I like working by myself because different people work in different ways.		1
I prefer to work in a pair	24%	5*
• I like to work in a pair because your partner can help you when you get stuck/because I get confused sometimes/sometimes I struggle on my own and I ask for help.		3
• Because you get help off the other person and you'll help them.		1
• Because a group is too loud and on my own is too hard.		1
I prefer to work in a group	43%	9*
• I like working in a group because we can share each other's ideas/because if you get stuck you have the rest of the group to help you work it out/work together to get the answer/talk about it.		8
• It's better to work in a group as it is easy.		1

Nearly half of Y4 preferred group work and all but one gave the same reason: to share ideas and support each other. It is difficult to hypothesise why there is such a big variation in preferences between children so close in age. The attitude difference could perhaps be simply down to the particular cohort of children or perhaps because children lack the skills for group work (Godhino and Shrimpton 2002). In both Y3 and Y4 the paired work was more effective (Fox 2005), as evidenced in transcript analyses in chapter five.

Children's Interview Groups

The discussions with children show that many children do not value speaking and listening. The children perceived reading and writing to be 'proper' work and tended not to choose speaking and listening as their favourite activity (see graph below). However, children seemed to struggle when asked to justify their choice.

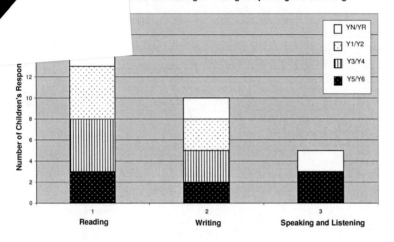

The interviews indicate that most favoured reading but few reasons were given, especially from the younger children. Some examples included: 'I like stories.' 'I prefer reading because you are writing and reading as well.' 'You are still reading but you don't have to use your hands.' 'I like reading because sometimes you can learn.' 'Just like it.' 'I like reading because I get into the story more.' 'Because when people make films about the stories, the stories include more ... like *Harry Potter*.'

The few reasons for writing being a favourite activity included: 'It's good writing about stuff.' 'I like writing because... I just like writing!' 'You don't have to discuss answers.' 'When you write you can just write what you think instead of talking to everyone about it.' 'So you can just write and show the teacher.'

Only a small minority chose speaking and listening and two groups, which represent four classes, did not choose it at all. However, more reasons were offered for selecting it, including: 'Because when you are listening to the people it's showing you what they thought of the question and you're giving what you thought and you can discuss it and work out the best answer for the question.' 'You don't have to just write everything down; you can tell everyone what you've got and what they've got.' 'If you don't like speaking you can listen to other people's answers.

The lack of value given to speaking and listening could come from a variety of sources, such as from the low status it is given in many in education policies (NLS, 1998); lack of staff training (Cameron QCA 2003c); staff are unwilling to let go of perceived control, so do not give children much opportunity to engage in speaking and listening (Edwards QCA 2003); perhaps teachers do not step back from scaffolding the process slowly enough to enable children to learn to use the appropriate skills independently (Palincsar and Brown 1985); lack of an adult facilitator who can intervene and scaffold the process (Harmon 2002).

Although most children favoured collaborative work, certain groups had the attitude that collaborative work was copying; that speaking and listening was not 'proper' work; and that the teacher was the only person worth asking because other children probably had the wrong answer anyway. Most groups, however, stressed the benefits of working together to share ideas; give or receive help when struggling with work; to find out different ways of working things out; and have the chance to work with friends.

The younger children liked speaking and listening activities because they saw it either as play or the opportunity to talk to their friends. The older children emphasised sharing ideas and learning from others. The children came up with more reasons why they did not like speaking and listening than positive ones. Most children, across all age groups, commented about the issue of noise; children shouting; and getting headaches. Some younger children did not like the fact that the teacher talked too much and that they spent too long on the carpet. The older children complained of being distracted; of others messing about; of people laughing if a mistake was made; and others copying their work and ideas.

The children said the types of speaking and listening activities were: listening to people talking or reading; working with a writing partner; talking to a partner and saying how to do the answer; cross-curricular links – using speaking in listening in other subjects, such as geography, or maths when discussing the problem and answers to the problems; in role play; when other work is finished; to try and ask a partner what they thought of each other's work.

This chart shows children's perceptions of how often they worked: alone, in pairs or in groups. It is interesting to compare this with the staff perception, on page 48.

Children's Interview Groups						
Yr group:	Combined total for **ALL** age groups (Foundation, KS1, Lower KS2, Upper KS2)					
		Every lesson	Every day	2 or 3 times a week	Once a week	Less than weekly
1	How often do you work on your own?	2	11	12	2	5
2	How often do you work in pairs?	1	14	5	4	8
3	How often do you work in groups?	0	10	7	5	10

Overall, it seems that children are taught in a variety of ways, but on a daily basis, rather than in each lesson. It may be significant that equal numbers of children perceived group work to be every day (10 responses) yet other children (again 10 responses) believed it to be less than weekly. This suggests that differences may be according to age group. It is, therefore, relevant to look at the charts for each interview group separately, as the data varies between the year groups.

Children's Interview Groups						
Age group:	**Foundation X** KS1			Lower KS2		Upper KS2
		Every lesson	Every day	2 or 3 times a week	Once a week	Less than weekly
1	How often do you work on your own?	1	1	1	0	5
2	How often do you work in pairs?	1	3	1	1	2
3	How often do you work in groups?	0	6	0	0	2

The separate pupil data shows that Foundation Stage children cited group work as most common (daily) and individual work as less than weekly.

Children's Interview Groups						
Age group:	Foundation	**KS1 X**		Lower KS2		Upper KS2
		Every lesson	**Every day**	**2 or 3 times a week**	**Once a week**	**Less than weekly**
1	How often do you work on your own?	1	5	1	1	0
2	How often do you work in pairs?	0	0	0	0	8
3	How often do you work in groups?	0	4	2	1	1

All KS1 responses were that paired work was done less than weekly, which is surprising, as class observations showed a high incidence of paired work and the children seemed used to working in this way. The common working pattern was deemed to be either individually or in groups.

Children's Interview Groups						
Age group:	Foundation	KS1		**Lower KS2 X**		Upper KS2
		Every lesson	**Every day**	**2 or 3 times a week**	**Once a week**	**Less than weekly**
1	How often do you work on your own?	0	5	3	0	0
2	How often do you work in pairs?	0	0	4	2	2
3	How often do you work in groups?	0	0	3	2	3

Lower KS2 highlighted individual work as the most usual way of working (every day) with paired and individual work being only 2 or 3 times a week. However, class observations showed that paired work was most common.

Children's Interview Groups							
Age group:		Foundation		KS1	Lower KS2		Upper KS2 X

		Every lesson	Every day	2 or 3 times a week	Once a week	Less than weekly
1	How often do you work on your own?	0	0	7	1	0
2	How often do you work in pairs?	0	7	0	0	1
3	How often do you work in groups?	0	0	2	2	4

Upper KS2 believed they worked predominantly in pairs, yet observations were all of group work. The children claimed working alone was the next most common way of learning, with group work being less frequent. The children's interviews generally confirmed results from the questionnaires, but differed in that more information was gained in the interviews about what the children did not like about speaking and listening or collaborative activities. Overall, children wanted the support that collaborative work gave them, but they were aware of the disadvantages, such as noise and copying. The majority felt it important to be able to choose who they worked with, as they found it hard to work with the teacher's choice, if they did not like who they had been paired or grouped with.

Staff Attitude ~ Staff Questionnaires

The questionnaires included the opinions of both the teachers and the support staff. This chart shows staff views of how often children work in pairs or groups, and can be compared with the previous charts showing children's perceptions.

Teacher & Support Staff Answers From staff questionnaire:		Every lesson	Every day	2 or 3 times a week	Once a week	Less than weekly
21	How often do you allow children to work in pairs?	6	4	2	1	0
22	How often do you allow children to work in groups?	5	7	0	0	2

Staff believe that collaborative work happens regularly, half of responses suggesting paired work is daily. In contrast, the children seem to feel that opportunities are fewer. The majority of staff claim paired or group work occurs either in every lesson or at least daily. It differs from the children's opinion in that 11 staff responses show that collaborative work of some kind takes place every lesson, whereas only 1 child out of 32 said this was the case.

The table, in appendix E2 p162, shows separate responses from teachers and support staff to the staff questionnaire. Clearly, there is consistency between views of teaching and support staff: the responses are usually in the same response category or at least paired in adjacent boxes, denoting the same positive or negative opinion. Having consistency between the views of teachers and support staff will probably lead to more success in implementing more speaking, listening and collaborative work.

The overall staff responses (see table below) show unanimous agreement that speaking and listening are just as important as reading and writing and are vital to promote reading and writing, with 12/15 in the agree strongly category for both question (1) and (2). Nearly all staff (14/15) believed that children enjoyed speaking and listening and preferred collaborative work. They also agreed that children benefit from working collaboratively with peers and that they have seen children supporting each others' learning. However, opinions differ on certain issues, such as in question (13) about whether or not there are sufficient resources. In question (5), 5 staff agree that they prefer children to work independently, whereas 10 disagree. There is an even split of opinions about whether children 'mess about' during speaking and listening activities, which confirms this to be an issue, despite the overall positive view and valuing of speaking and listening. This reflects the view that suggests children tend to have little experience of listening to each other because teachers worry about the risks of noise and losing classroom control (Edwards, QCA 2003c).

Results from Staff Questionnaire.				

Teachers and Support Staff – combined figures.	Agree strongly	Agree	Disagree	Disagree strongly
1 Speaking and listening are just as important as reading and writing.	12	3		
2 Speaking and listening are vital to promote reading and writing.	12	3		
3 Speaking and listening activities are difficult to manage.	1	9	4	
4 Children enjoy speaking and listening activities.	5	9	1	
5 Children prefer to work in pairs or groups, rather than on their own.	5	8	2	
6 I would prefer children to work independently.		5	9	1
7 Children mess about during speaking and listening activities.		7	7	1
8 Children benefit from working collaboratively with their peers.	8	7		
9 Children complete tasks better when they work with others.	2	9	3	
10 I have seen children supporting each others' learning.	10	3		
11 I have received enough training for promoting speaking and listening.		5	10	
12 I would like to receive more training for promoting speaking and listening.	8	6		1
13 I have a range of resources for promoting speaking and listening.		6	7	1
14 I plan specifically for speaking and listening activities.	4	9	1	
15 I only teach speaking and listening in literacy.		1	7	6
16 I teach speaking and listening in many curricular subjects.	8	6		
17 I encourage the children to work in pairs.	7	8		
18 I encourage the children to work in groups.	8	7		
19 Children still record their work individually even if they do a task in groups.	5	5	4	
20 I find speaking and listening difficult to assess.	1	9	4	

No response given to certain questions.	Every lesson	Every day	2 or 3 times a week	Once a week	Less than weekly
21 How often do you allow children to work in pairs?	6	4	2	1	
22 How often do you allow children to work in groups?	5	7			2

Two thirds of staff (10/15) claim not to have received enough training and all but one (a teacher) confirm they require more. This matches Cameron's view that teachers are not supported adequately with the curriculum (Cameron, in QCA 2003c). It is significant that it was mainly teachers (7/8) who felt they had not had sufficient training, unlike support staff who were evenly split. The other area staff were negative about was that speaking and listening activities are difficult to manage (10/15 in question 3) and 7/15 confirming that children tend to mess about. Despite this, 11/15 agreed, (2 agreeing strongly), that children complete tasks better when they work with others.

Virtually all staff claim to plan specifically for speaking and listening and 14/15 teach it in other curricular subjects, but they find it hard to assess, as is noted in the open-ended questions (23 and 24) related below. All 15 staff agree they encourage the children to work in pairs and in groups, with half (8) agreeing strongly. Despite this, 10 responded that they would still want children to record their work individually, even if they do a task in groups. This would seem to indicate that collaborative work is not valued as a means of obtaining a group process, product or decision. It could also work against one of the benefits of collaborative work – that less able writers can contribute without being hampered by poor transcription skills.

Overall, staff agree that speaking, listening and collaborative skills are valued for supporting children's learning but that there are difficulties with management and assessment. There were also 2 open-ended questions, plus a space for other comments, which are summarised here, but a full transcript is in appendix, D4 p153. More teachers than support staff filled out these questions, but many comments reflected the same issues. So what now follows is a summary of responses to the open-ended questions.

Qu 23: What are the positive and negative aspects of speaking and listening, for the teacher and for the children?
For teachers, speaking and listening activities can be difficult to manage with a class that cannot settle or who are lively. Children may just chat about things other than work and classes could become noisy. Though valid points can be made about a particular topic it is much harder to record evidence of knowledge for assessment. However, speaking and listening activities can give the teacher the chance to re-direct any misunderstandings; to establish children's knowledge if they are not able to express themselves through writing;

and allow them to learn things about quieter children who are unwilling to converse with adults.

For children, speaking and listening can be difficult, as some find it hard to communicate and struggle to listen or see the viewpoint of others. The less confident children can be dominated by louder children and teachers may not be there to redress the balance. However, children benefit by discussing work and sharing ideas or experiences; by having the chance to think things through first before embarking on written tasks; and by being able to get across ideas without the barrier of having to write it down. It facilitates learning to take turns; sharing responsibility; problem-solve; and also builds the confidence of shyer children.

Qu 24 What are the benefits and disadvantages of children working collaboratively, for the teacher and for the children?

For the teacher, it can be difficult to keep children on task during collaborative work and at times it seems that not a lot of work is completed. Some children will not, or maybe cannot, contribute, which can lead to children copying others' work without understanding it. However, it can be easier to organise a group than a whole class in terms of time and resources. Also, collaborative tasks can lead to a blossoming of ideas and the possibility of more actual written work being recorded: 'two heads better than one' idea (Mercer 2000)

Some children find it difficult to collaborate with others, perhaps because they cannot listen; while others simply prefer to work on their own, and not join in. Less confident children may be over-ruled by more dominant peers or quiet children may go unnoticed because of loud chatter; and less able children may just copy others' work. However, collaborative activities can teach children to listen and respond to others; enable less confident children to be supported by their peers; lead to children discussing work with each other and therefore understand it better; facilitate the exchange of ideas, which can be combined and lead to better outcomes; foster more active and interesting lessons; and develop confidence to present ideas.

Other comments section.

This included using philosophical enquiry to help children really listen to each other; consider others' ideas; and to express their thoughts and feelings in words. It was also pointed out that the learning environment itself, such a classroom size and organisation, can dictate the success or failure of collaborative activities. Talk can be used for sharing observations, giving advice and justifying decisions, yet still include times where children are perceived to be off-task and chatting about issues in their lives (Gustafson and MacDonald, 2004). Furthermore, each child needs to be guided to find best way of learning for them. Finally, young children need an extensive vocabulary before they can learn to read or write successfully (Hohmann 2005). The two open-questions and other comments section reflect and enhance the questionnaire responses discussed earlier. They also enabled staff that weren't interviewed the opportunity to make further comments.

Staff Interviews

Staff interviews confirmed the questionnaire findings: demonstrating a high commitment and positive attitude for collaborative work; and for promoting a range of speaking and listening opportunities across the curriculum. However, staff were also realistic about some of the limitations: such as lack of training and children going off task. Staff did recognise the important role of talk, reflecting Czerniewska's view (1992), that even in a society with a written culture, speaking is the most frequent activity for virtually all individuals. At the same time, there was consensus that speaking and listening received less emphasis than reading and writing, particularly in the junior age group and was influenced by not being directly tested. There was awareness that language is communication, which varies according to children's cultural differences, as exemplified by Ivanicō (2003), and the teachers did take into account a child's personal, social, cultural and economic, background. Staff were unanimous in highlighting issues of poor language development of some children on entering their nursery and that the children were rarely spoken to at home and that parents did not elaborate their speech (McClelland 2002). This put pressure on the school to close this language delay gap, by focussing on language and vocabulary extension.

There were some concerns over how to plan and teach speaking and listening effectively but most concern arose about how to assess it effectively. Staff believe they encouraged children to work collaboratively by either expecting it as a matter of course, and some gave specific instructions to work either in pairs or groups. The Foundation teacher observed that at times children may appear to be working together but were, in actual fact, working alongside each other. The issue here was that it depended on the child's stage of development. This collaborative work was used in all subjects, and not confined to literacy.

53

All staff were clear that collaborative work supported task completion for many children, but that some children genuinely preferred to work on their own. They were keen to accommodate children's individual needs and also felt that there were times where collaboration could be a hindrance. There was unanimous agreement that children could support each other's learning:

> **Foundation:** children 'given confidence, and it gives them a forum to speak where they probably wouldn't in a different situation.'
>
> **KS1:** 'it can help formulate their ideas.'
>
> **Lower KS2:** 'more able ones can support the less able by talking to them about it...'
>
> **Upper KS2:** 'they can give advice and give ideas...'

All staff wanted more training in the form of videos; seeing others teach; room on planning forms specifically for speaking and listening; team teaching; 'expert' advice; seeing a plan and then the actual lesson; having a colleague to help with assessment. It appeared that there was little formal planning for speaking and listening and that assessment was 'in the head'. This was is contrast to planning and assessment for reading and writing, which was formalised. Foundation and KS1 staff seemed to do more 'modelling' or demonstration to children of how to speak and how to listen, particularly through teacher involvement in role-play. There was more organisation for oral activities with younger children but the older children were set targets by one teacher for oral presentation and another teacher modelled appropriate responses to questions.

Three teachers pointed out that collaborative work enabled them to listen to the children talking to each other about their learning, enabling the teacher to know if the children had understood and to intervene where there were misunderstandings. Although all staff saw benefits of speaking and listening to improve reading and writing, junior staff in particular felt under pressure to have written evidence of work. All were committed to practical activities and building children's confidence; fostering paired work or response partners or setting group tasks. All teachers used discussion and problem-solving across different subjects and 'hot seating' (questioning) to develop an understanding of character. Staff all commented that neither the Foundation Stage Curriculum nor the National Literacy Strategy gave enough support and guidance to teach speaking and listening effectively. There was a feeling that oracy needed to be given more status and that if it were promoted in all age groups, that children would develop better skills in oracy, reading and writing.

They felt that teachers and trainee teachers needed to know more about how to promote collaborative work.

Supplementary questions and comments highlighted the need to link subjects together and plan where speaking and listening can be promoted specifically and explicitly in certain topics and implicitly in others. The importance of transition was highlighted and that staff should be more aware of the strategies and materials being used in different year groups: to share resources and ideas. There was still concern about how to fit oracy into an already packed curriculum, where children still needed to write and read and do handwriting plus the pressure of Ofsted inspections and feeling the need to justify speaking and listening activities. There was also an issue over formal versus informal work in the early years and how children were still expected to begin formal work when they were not ready. The staff were keen to meet the children's developmental needs but felt pressure to begin formal schooling to match government policy. They also felt that many parents were unable to support their children at home and this led to children falling further behind.

The staff interviews confirmed the comments and replies from the questionnaires but differed from them in that more detailed information was gained about the management of speaking and listening and the pressures on staff. Obviously there is no data here from support staff here. Overall, there was a clear desire to promote collaborative work and oracy, evidence that elements were already in place, but that some difficulties and barriers were hindering full implementation.

Summary of Staff and Pupil Attitudes
Both pupils and staff felt positive about speaking and listening but staff were more aware of the value to learning. However there were some differences in opinion, in that children perceived there to be less opportunity for collaborative work than staff. Common themes were that collaborative work increased confidence and sharing of ideas but that it could be noisy and distracting. It was recognised that collaborative work should be promoted but that there were times when it was inappropriate. Interviews gave a more detailed picture of both attitudes and what was happening in the school: confirming and extending the questionnaires.

Opportunities for collaborative work through talk

The information on child and teacher attitudes to collaborative work and the number of minutes in each lesson will now be supplemented with observation notes and transcripts of child-to-child recordings of talk and interaction. It will also include whether the class teacher gave explicit permission for the children to work together. The staff perceptions, discussed earlier, showed that collaborative work was occurring at least daily and many suggested in each lesson. The previously described children's views were that collaborative work did happen but not in every lesson, many suggesting daily, but others only on a weekly basis. Staff and pupil attitudes and practice showed collaborative work taking place. The next chapter, discourse analysis of observation transcripts, will examine the quality of peer talk and collaboration.

Chapter Five: Findings and Discussion of Results
~ Discourse Analysis Data

The other three objectives for the research project are: to analyse the types and quality of talk (Francis and Hunston 1998); to investigate whether opportunities for paired or group talk support or hinder task completion; and to look for evidence of pupils scaffolding each other's learning (Palinscar and Brown 1985, Harmon 2002, Rojas-Drummond 2000 and Mattos 2000). These are closely linked and all require data from the discourse analysis. I propose, therefore, to examine the dialogue transcripts from each class separately and consider the remaining three objectives for each class at the same time. I shall analyse the dialogues chronologically by children's age and then draw together common elements from each year group in another section. This section will consider each of the remaining objectives separately, but include an overall impression from all classes.

Full transcripts for all year groups are in appendix D1 p97 and my own analysis within the transcripts is in **bold**.

Nursery
Background information: the lesson involved one task lasting 20 minutes. The teacher is introducing a new role play area and spent 30 minutes as a whole class suggesting vocabulary relating to garages, building on the previous day when she had shown the children around her car. McClelland (2002) highlights teachers' concerns that more children are arriving into nursery with poorer language skills; a less well developed vocabulary and a reduced capacity to listen. As it was a new role play, the teacher prompted by modelling appropriate vocabulary, sentences and phrases, but the children were still interacting with each other, so the session has been considered as peer talk.

Godhino and Shrimpton (2002) found that children with ESL (English as a second language) and children from lower socioeconomic backgrounds gave particularly short answers. This is confirmed in Hicks's (1995) examination of Heath's (1982/1983) studies on restricted speech in white working class families. The children in my observation generally use short utterances, such as:

Owen:	The wheel's broke.
Fred:	I need the <tools>.
Susan:	I'm on the road.

Therefore, the teacher is scaffolding the children, by modelling the appropriate language and vocabulary as advocated by Bruner (1978, in Lillis and McKinney 2003) and Palincsar and Brown (1985), so the children have a better idea of how to act and what to say:

Giles:	My car's broke.
Teacher:	Can you fix it straight away or does he have to come back later? The garage looks a bit full.
Fred:	Do you want me to fix that? I can do it now or bring it back later.

It is clear that Fred has responded to the teacher's prompt by using the vocabulary modelled by the teacher, forming longer sentences.

The children tend to respond to teacher prompts more than to each other. However, there are times when they interact with each other, often in pairs rather than groups. There is collaboration but little dialogue.

Giles:	((*Breaks down*))
Susan&Owen:	((*Go for petrol*))
Matthew:	I need a hammer.
Owen:	My petrol cap is this way.
Fred:	((*Hammers Giles' car*))
Simon:	((*Pretends to put oil in Susan's car*))

These are young children who would typically display solitary or parallel play, so the role play process is aiming to get them to work collaboratively and develop their language skills. There are times when children speak in longer sentences, but these are rare.

Generally, the children are relying on the teacher to organise the role play and offer suggestions, which match the children's linguistic and social development. This links to the work of Harmon (2002) on reading, where she examines how peer talk can support learners, but stresses how an adult facilitator is needed to intervene and scaffold the process. The talk is mainly cumulative (Mercer 2000), as talk is simply reaffirmed rather than questioned and developed. The task needs collaborative work, so the fact children were in a group was essential. The teacher was providing the scaffolding for this task, as the children have not yet developed the appropriate skills to do this for each other (Palincsar and Brown, 1985).

Reception

Background information: the lesson involved one group task lasting 20 minutes. My comments during all of the remaining YR-Y6 transcriptions are in **bold**. During group and independent work time, after the whole class input session, the teacher explicitly told the children to talk about work to each other. This group had to make story characters from 'We're going on a bear Hunt' out of play dough, place the characters on the story map and retell the story together.

Lucy tries to set out the parts of the story by asking others to help her with what comes next:

Lucy:	What comes after the dirty dirty dirty dirty mud? **Aiming for a sequence/prompt.**
	~ ~ ~ ~ ~
Lucy:	What's coming next? The forest? **Asks for guidance again.**
Ruby:	I'm doing the forest.
Helen:	I'm doing the forest.
Alice:	I've done my forest. **No collaboration, all doing their own work.**

Alice also tries to keep the momentum going, by reminding the others that they need to re-tell the story:

Alice:	Let's tell the story now. **At last, someone remembers the task.**
	~ ~ ~ ~ ~
Alice:	If everybody's done it you've got to tell the story now. **Task reminder again from Alice.**

The type of talk is partly disputational (Mercer 2000), as there are moments of friction:

Jane:	Let everybody finish first.
Lucy:	We've already finished.
Ruby:	Ha ha I beat Jane.
Helen:	No you haven't, you haven't done the water.

and partly cumulative, where children agree with the answer just given by another child:

Lucy:	Everything is squashy. **'Squashy' as in the book.**
Jane:	Squashy. **Repeats Lucy.**
Lucy:	I'm making I'm making grass.
Helen:	((*Singing*)) I'm making grass. **Repeats Lucy.**

The children did not complete the task fully, but talked about random bits of the story or repeated onomatopoeic words, such as:

Lucy:	Oozy mud. [later on] Squelch squirch.

There was some evidence of pupils scaffolding each other's learning (Gustafson and MacDonald 2004):

Lucy:	What comes after the dirty dirty dirty dirty mud? **Aiming for a sequence/prompt.**
Helen:	A snowstorm. Mine's squishy. **Support given.**
Lucy:	Where's the snowstorm? **Supplementary question asking for clarification.**

There is no evidence of exploratory talk (Mercer 2000); there is no real development of ideas. Working as a group may have been of some help, in that children reminded each other of what other parts of the story they needed to create. However, it could also be seen as a hindrance, as much time was spent just 'playing' with the play-dough. Perhaps if the children had been set the task in pairs, recommended by Fox (2005) as being more effective than most group work, more would have achieved. The story does not really get re-told, just odd bits mentioned at random. The children focus more on manipulating the play dough than sequencing and retelling the story, as instructed. However, from the vocabulary they are using, they have remembered parts of the story.

Year 1

Background information: the lesson involved 4 separate activities, mainly in pairs, lasting between 2 and 20 minutes. In activity one (10 minutes) the teacher explicitly told the children to work in pairs for their phonics (filling in a phonemes frame), to take turns to scribe on a white board. She gave a clear explanation of how to work together and why this was beneficial for the children (talk to each other and decide what to write).

Teacher:	First word is an easy one, it's man, <u>man</u>.
Carl:	'm' you want an 'm' **Offers suggestion.**
Rob:	((*Writes 'm' Carl watches*)) **Rob is the scribe for the 1st word.**
Carl:	'a' **Offers the next letter.**
Rob:	((*Writes 'a'*)) **Scribes.**
Carl:	That's a 'n' **Suggests final letter.**
Rob:	'm' ((*Writes 'm'*)) **Makes a mistake.**
Carl:	<u>'n'</u> at the end. **Peer scaffolding.**

There is clear evidence here that the children are working co-operatively, by taking turns to be the scribe and to offer spelling suggestions. They are also scaffolding each other's learning by either correcting each other's mistakes or by prompting to show there is an error and letting their partner correct it themselves (Gustafson and MacDonald, 2004).

In activity two (2 minutes), the whole class were on the carpet and the teacher explicitly told the children to discuss a recount, in pairs.

((*Whispering to each other, too quiet to hear first few sentences*))	
Mandy:	They went to the fire station.
Zoe:	A big place.
Mandy:	They sat by the wheel.
Zoe:	Remember a man read a story and he jumped off and drawed a picture.
Mandy:	He went up a pole.
Zoe:	And grabbed it dead quick.

The children jogged each other's memories by each contributing their own recollections. However, the final result of the set task was that although they remembered elements, they did not coherently recount the story. Perhaps they needed longer to piece their recollections together.

In activity three (also 2 minutes) the teacher explicitly told the children to work, together to sequence events.

Molly:	erm what it's about is they went to get ice cream.
Jade:	((*Laughing*)) The bouncy castle and got some ice cream. **Jade builds on Molly's contribution.**
Molly:	He might have gone the shops then. Ha! There's the mike. ((*Pointing at the microphone*)) **Distracted by research process.**
Jade:	erm (5) He went to the Isle of Man.
Molly:	Bouncy castle, ice cream and the shop. **Lists elements.**
Jade:	Er a man went on the pulley.
Molly:	A little boy went on the pulley. **Corrects Jade.** If you want it to go up you have to pull it that way, if you want to go down you let go of it a bit of the time.

This is similar to the other activity, where the task is not completed properly but each child remembers something, which is built on by the other.

In the fourth activity (20 minutes), the teacher explicitly told the children to work together to explain, by taking turns to write sentences, what is happening in some photographs related to the fire station open day. Although the children are taking turns to write in pairs, the group below often refer to each other's work, so the whole group has been transcribed.

Paula:	What's that there?
Judy:	Look it's a microphone.
Adrian:	It's in the middle.
	(*Paula singing in background ah ah ah ah ah ah ah*)
	Distracted by research process.
Amber:	They're just photographs.
Paula:	[What shall we write? **Tries to get on with task, asks for help.**
Tony:	Pass me that pencil.]
Judy:	The boy went to the Isle of Man ((*Replies to Paula*)).
	((*Paula chanting in background yeah yeah yeah yeah yeah yeah*))
Amber:	Yeah.
Judy:	((*Writing one word at a time as she said them aloud*)) The-boy-went-to-the-Isle-of-Man. **On task.**
Amber:	[In the summer I went on holiday.
Adrian:	It's a girl.] ((*Referring to Judy's comment*))
Paula:	No.
Adrian:	The one in the green jacket is the boy. **Corrects Judy.**

This could be considered disputational talk (Mercer, 2000), but generally they engage in cumulative talk, making suggestions for what they should write. Occasionally they are involved in a basic level of exploratory talk, when they make different suggestions and decide on one, but there is little discussion of reasons for choice. There is a feeling here that children hold each other responsible for taking part in the work (Sullivan 2002). It could be simply down to whom is more dominant, but the children do offer each other help including suggestions and spelling support. Therefore, there is evidence of peer scaffolding of each other's learning. Some group members, such as Judy and Adrian, could have got more work done by not supporting those who needed help. However, they seemed to feel that they were not competing with each other, but trying to work together. Sullivan (2002) and Gustafson and MacDonald (2004) point out that children can do what is required of them, even though they may, at times, drift off-task, as exemplified in this case.

Year 2
Background information: the lesson involved 4 separate activities, 3 in pairs and 1 in a group, lasting between 1 and 15 minutes. In activity one (1 minute) the teacher explicitly told the children to work in pairs to discuss suitable questions for a selection of headings (communicating, playing, keeping clean, eating, sleeping, moving) to ask the mums, who were due to come into school.

Barry:	How do babies communicate?
Stuart:	They're copying ours. **More concerned about another pair.**
Barry:	What do babies eat? **Comes up with a second question.**
Stuart:	So, you're doing that one (5) you're only meant to do one. **Still more concerned with other things and has made no contribution.**
Barry:	Blah blah blah blah.
Stuart:	erm.
Barry:	You do one. **Tries to make Stuart take a turn.**
Stuart:	Why do babies sleep?

This is a very short activity where Barry does more work than Stuart, who is distracted and off task. Eventually he is forced by Barry to make a contribution. This reflects Sullivan's findings (2002), who notes children hold each other accountable and expect each other to contribute work.

In this second 5 minute activity, the teacher explicitly told the children to work with their writing partner (sharing a white board and taking turns to write) to make a question they could ask the mums, who were due to come into school.

Norman:	He's not letting me work with him. ((*Turning to teacher*)) **A tense start.**
George:	I am. ((*Gives Norman the Whiteboard*))
Norman:	When do babies usually communicate? ((*Starts writing it down*)) **Thinks of question and starts to write it down.**
George:	((*Spells out word*)) B-A-B-Y NO I-E-S C-O-M-M-U-N-I-C-A-T-E **Helps Norman by sounding out spellings.**
Norman:	You need to write a question. **Wants George to think of a question.**
George:	((*starts to write*)) How do babies eat? ((*Norman watches George write*)) ((*Another child accuses this pair of copying*))
Norman:	We've done our own question, not yours ((*Turning to another pair*))
George:	Shall we do another one? **On task.**

This exchange is strange because there is tension between them at several points, which might have prevented task completion (disputational talk). However, both are keen to do more questions and they correct or support each other, where necessary.

This third task lasted less than a minute. The teacher explicitly told children to work together and choose one question the pair would like to ask the mums.

Ben:	My question.
Roger:	No mine.
Ben:	Mine's better.
Roger:	No I'm having my question.

The teacher stopped the class because too many children were arguing. It seems that they lacked the negotiation skills to select a question, each wanting their question to be chosen. This could confirm the view of Edwards (QCA 2003), who advocates that children's limited experience of listening to each other, due to teachers worrying about losing classroom control, prevents children learning higher oracy skills.

The final task (15 minutes) is during the independent/group work part of the lesson. The teacher asked the children to work in groups with flip chart paper and markers. Each table had its own heading and they had to devise questions for the mums of a baby and a toddler on their heading.

Tom:	When does Brenda go?
Bill:	My turn after you.
Brenda:	Why don't you do one? (15) When do babies bath? ((*Tom writes the question*))
Mabel:	How do babies keep clean? ((*Starts to write*))
Tom:	Write yours there. ((*Pointing to the sheet*))
Bill:	Hurry up. It's my turn after you. **Tension.**
Tom:	No it goes round in a circle. **Tension.**
Bill:	Okay. It's me after. **Tension.**
Brenda:	My turn after you. **Tension.**
Bill:	Your handwriting's small. **Tension.**
Brenda:	I like Tom's handwriting.
Tom:	Ah. Look what you've done. ((*Bill had grabbed pen and written on Tom's jumper*)) **Tension.**
Mabel:	When do babies have their ((*Tom interrupts*)) **Tries a question.**
Tom:	How do babies keep their teeth clean?
Brenda:	Put a question mark. **Prompts.**
Mabel:	It's like this. ((*Points at one*)) **Helps.**

There is a fair amount of tension and argument, leading to a lack of productivity typical of disputational talk. There are also many occasions where children are off task and not even engaging in the cumulative talk, which covers the remaining dialogue. This is shown where children don't productively question each other and explain choices, but come up with some work, but not of as high a quality as it could have been with a better discussion. Group work and talk, in this case, was more of a hindrance than the small amount of help they gave each other. This concurs with the work of Fox (2005) who advocates that even adults lack the skills to work in groups of over 4 people.

Year 3

Background information: the lesson was based on a poem - *Custard the Dragon*. There were 4 tasks lasting between 2 and 20 minutes. In the first 2 minute activity, the teacher explicitly told children to work with the person next to them, to clap and count syllables on line one of the poem.

Jess:	Syllables.
Olivia:	((*Sings and claps first line*)) Be-lin-da lives in a little white house
Jess:	No **Disagrees.**
Olivia:	9 syllables (.) put 9
Jess:	There's 2 in little (5) ((*Claps*)) lit-tle there's 2 in little **Corrects Olivia.**
Olivia:	((*Recites again*)) Be-lin-da lives in a lit-tle white house **Gets it right.**
Jess:	There's 10 **Correct answer through peer support.**

Jess helps Olivia, by showing her the syllables in 'little' by clapping it. Olivia then has a go herself and gets it right, which shows successful peer scaffolding.

This next excerpt (activity two) is the same task as the last one, but with the second line of the poem.

Peter:	We do the second line now.
Alan:	with is 1 syllable.
Peter:	((*Reads words*)) with a little black kitten and a little grey mouse.
Alan:	((*Claps along with Peter's reciting*)) **Collaborating.**
Peter:	with 1 a 1 little 1 black 1 kit-ten 2 and 1 a 1 little 1 grey 1 mouse 1
Alan:	lit-tle is 2 ((*Claps twice for little*)) **Helps and corrects.** What's the answer to that?
Peter:	1 2 3 4 5 6 7 8 9 10 11 12 13 (5) There's 13.
Alan:	((*Checks himself*)) with 1 a 1 lit-tle 2 black 1 kit-ten 2 and 1 a 1 lit-tle 2 grey 1 mouse 1 **Makes sure the answer is correct.**
Peter:	Do we do the third line now?
Alan:	Don't do that line yet.

Again, working as a pair was beneficial to complete the task correctly. (Fox 2005).

This is the latter part of task 3, to do the next 2 lines of the poem, but shows how easily children can become distracted.

Jemma:	Drag-on drag-on rea-li-o tru-li-o
Anna:	So 1,2,3,4,5,6,7,8,9,10,11,12
Jemma:	No.
Anna:	12, 12
Jemma:	We're done then.
	((*Another teacher comes into the class*))
Anna:	HOORAY Here's Mr Atkinson. **Off task.**
Jemma:	I want to go to the tennis (5) tennis. **Off task.**
	(*Teacher went through the third and fourth lines, then moved on to looking at rhyming couplets*)

The children had been on task before the other teacher came in, but then did not complete their activity.

The fourth and final activity (20 minutes) was to look at rhyming couplets. There are things that prevent children from working, usually minor things, but that are nevertheless disruptive.

Stephen:	Where's the pencil? **Things that delay children from working.**
Lisa:	There's none in there. ((*Stephen goes off to find a pencil*))
	~ ~ ~ ~ ~
Rhiannon:	Has anyone got a sharpener? **Again, not having equipment to hand, wastes work time.**

This group task also shows moments of tension.

Lisa:	How come you keep writing it Stephen?
Stephen:	YOU'RE WRITING IT aren't ya? **Tension.**
	~ ~ ~ ~ ~
Derek:	Don't write it yet because we're all working together. Don't Stephen. **Tension.**
Lisa:	What are you doing Stephen? (5) **Tension.**
	~ ~ ~ ~ ~
Stephen:	Don't write it yet. **Dominates again.**
Derek:	Why? **Tension.**
Lisa:	Wait wait. **Tension.**

Although this could be disputational talk (Mercer 2000), which is unproductive, the group do get their work done. This is mainly through cumulative talk where they confirm each other's views without challenge but there is also a sequence of exploratory talk (at a basic level), where group members offer different answers and try to justify their choice to the others. Harmon (2002) suggests peer support can enhance learning through participants engaging in meaningful dialogues.

Derek:	The Gingerbread Boy was very
Stephen:	Very what Derek?
Lisa:	The Gingerbread Boy was very <u>sad</u>. It's not very bad it's very sad.
Stephen:	Does anyone think the gingerbread boy was a sneak?
Rhiannon:	No, I think he's very clever.
Stephen:	Does anyone think he ran away, and his mum was (5) erm, no no (.) he was very t?
Derek:	No
Stephen:	The gingerbread boy was very clever.

Rojas-Drummond (2000) and Mattos (2000), outline how either an adult expert or more knowledgeable peer can move learning on. Generally, working as a group supported rather than hindered task completion, as children did support each other, but pairs might have been a way of getting more work done with less tension. Gibbs (1994) comments teams need clear roles and need to be firm with each other on deadlines. Working in this way needs practice and the teacher needs to model and scaffold the process initially.

Year 4

Background: there are 4 activities based around a persuasive writing poster, 3 of them lasting 1 minute and one of 15 minutes. In the first, the teacher explicitly told the children to work in pairs to predict what the poster was about from looking at the pictures.

Carl:	It's about litter, like a litter bug.
Emma:	It could be about someone writing a letter and not knowing what to write.
Carl:	I've got a desk like that. **Not relevant to task.**
Emma:	Someone erm wrote a letter and threw it in the bin.
Carl:	It's about recycling.
Emma:	It could be about making things, there's card and paper and stuff.

In such a short activity, the children came up with a range of reasonable suggestions. In the second, the teacher explicitly told the children to work in pairs to decide what persuasion is.

Sean:	When you want someone to do something like save trees
Kelly:	But you need trees to help you live like oxygen.
Sean:	But nature's done that.
Kelly:	It's like, you want someone to do something like save trees so you try to persuade them to do what you want.
Sean:	It's like when you try to make someone do something.

Again, in a short activity the children fulfil the task. In the third activity, the teacher explicitly told the children to work in pairs on facts and opinions.

Amy:	A fact is like on the news.
Ian:	Facts are something that does happen.
Amy:	So many stuff in books.
Ian:	Like in science.
Amy:	I'm happy is my opinion.
Ian:	It's a way of looking at it.

Once again, the children work together to formulate an answer, building on each other's contributions, as in cumulative talk (Mercer 2000). The first 3 activities show cumulative talk and that paired work has been successful in supporting learning and task completion (Fox 2005).

The teacher, in the fourth task of 15 minutes, asked the children to identify, the opening statement, argument and closing statement in a photocopied piece of persuasive text, marking each with different coloured crayons. They also had to pick out 2 key points in the argument. Initially the teacher did not mention working collaboratively but after 2 minutes told them they could work with each other. For this task, the children worked in groups, rather than in pairs. As with one of the Y3 activities, there was time wasted on inconsequential matters.

Wendy:	((Rattling crayons)) What colours do we use?
Alan:	Doesn't matter.
Colin:	What's the title?
Wendy:	Pass me the blue.
Harry:	Sugar's bad for your teeth.
Alan:	Do you have to write in the middle?
Colin:	You have to write.
Alan:	Just get different colours.

In the next excerpt, the children are trying to work out what an argument is and what a conclusion is.

Wendy:	Harry, tell us what conclusion means.
Alan:	A bit of help please if you know what conclusion means.
Harry:	It's when some has had an argument.
Wendy:	It's like stopping an argument.
Alan:	Or it's the person that told you something.
Colin:	How do you spell it?
Wendy:	I'll have to read some of this.
Harry:	That's information.
Wendy:	((*Constant noise from banging and dropping crayons and pencils*))
Alan:	Put a question mark.
Colin:	I think I know what the whole argument is.

They cannot agree about what each bit is, although Harry and Colin work out the key message from the text. The whole dialogue with this group involves some disagreements but mainly being off task, worrying about the colours of crayons, finding rubbers and sharpeners. Working as a group has hindered task completion, as they do not achieve the objectives set by the teacher. Godhino and Shrimpton (2002) found that group work was poor, as many children lack social and cooperative skills. Also, children can be unclear what constitutes an effective discussion.

Year 5

Background: the lesson comprised 3 group activities based around *Charlotte's Webb* lasting 5, 10 and 15 minutes. In the first, the teacher explicitly told the children to discuss vocabulary in groups and decide whether it was 1950s, American or simply unfamiliar to them.

James:	Papa.
Sophie:	That's the Spanish word for Dad.
Megan:	And sneakers.
Beth:	Pop or Pops.
Megan:	I've never heard of Papa.
Beth:	There's this little girl in our Morris Dancing, right =
James:	Blissful.
Beth:	= and she calls him Pops.
James:	Specimen.
Megan:	I've never heard of that.
Sophie:	I have.

They managed to identify unfamiliar vocabulary and tell each other when it was not actually unfamiliar ie one may have heard of a word that the others had not, but were unable to categorise it, as the task required.

In the second activity, the teacher explicitly told the children to discuss 2 different viewpoints/persuasive arguments (for and against killing the pig), refer to text and write notes on white boards. Although they were told to work in pairs, they worked as a group.

Sarah:	Are you listening to this? I think that Fern should not keep the pig.
David:	The Dad's a trouble maker, that's what he thinks.
Jenny:	He's not a trouble maker, the pig is too small.
Sarah:	Like a baby.
Rachel:	I'm not messing.
Julie:	Read it here, too small and could die anyway.
David:	I'm sure it says trouble maker round here.
Jenny:	Whenever she's made a point I wrote it down.
Rachel:	Let Fern look after the pig.
David:	She's linking between her and the pig and she doesn't want the pig to be killed, she makes her points and has a persuasive argument.
Jenny:	If Fern was small, would her father kill her?

The children are working well at this point and offering different character's points of view, based on the text. They are also justifying their viewpoints, which points towards exploratory talk (Mercer 2000). However, they do go off task later.

Sarah:	It's maths next.
David:	I like maths, maths is gonna get me in to the Bluecoat.
Sarah:	Do you want to go to the Bluecoat?
David:	It's a good school. If you want to be a councillor and get to the top.

~ ~ ~ ~ ~

Jenny:	I'm having a pool party this year for my birthday, or a gym party. We want to book this gym thing for tomorrow for an hour.
David:	We're supposed to be working.

In the final task, the teacher explicitly told the children work together to do a role-play showing the character's opposing viewpoints. (Told to work in pairs but neither boy would role-play the female character, so teacher asked a girl to join them).

Eric:	Control yourself Fern.
Andrew:	Sobbing and pleading.
Eric:	You don't go 'sobbing and pleading'. **Critical, but correct, you don't read out the stage direction, but simply sob and plead.**
Andrew:	I want to be Mr Arable **Disagreement and a delaying tactic.** ((*Teacher asks girl to join the pair to play Fern*))
Eric:	She's Fern.
Andrew:	Did you do any planning for Fern?
Hazel:	I was going to be the pig. **Being awkward, she knows the teacher told her to play Fern.**
Andrew:	I want to play the pig or Mr Arable.

This first part goes well, with the children taking on the character roles based on the text. It is unfortunate that Hazel is so disparaging about the boys' efforts.

Eric:	Control yourself.
Hazel:	Control myself, this is a matter of life and death and you tell me to control myself.
Eric:	I can handle pigs better than you.
Hazel:	I know more about raising a litter of pigs than you do.
Eric:	But I'm a farmer.
Hazel:	So I'm younger. I'm little and you're big and I'm right and you're wrong and there's nothing you can do about it.
Eric:	It's my pig and I'm faster and you're slower.

Again, the next part goes well, but Andrew is critical.

| Andrew: | That wasn't good ((*Blows a raspberry*)). |

Although they play the character roles well, as a group outside the role play, they are using disputational talk. They are unnecessarily critical of each other's contributions. Overall in this class, there was some evidence of pupils scaffolding each other's learning, particularly in the paired work. The last activity showed they were prone to be critical of each other in an unproductive way. Corden (2000) recommends that teachers need to discuss ground rules with students, to ensure that productive collaborative discussions take place, rather than negative criticism. However, all the tasks showed positive elements and despite children going off task at times, were generally completed.

Year 6

Background information – The lesson is based on writing an introduction for a book review of *The Giant's Necklace:* (one task lasting 15 minutes). The teacher was on supply and had been there for 2 weeks, after a succession of different supply teachers, who could not control the class. He had never tried paired or group work, as the class was hard to manage, a factor Edwards (QCA 2003) cites, as preventing teachers trying collaborative work. Today was the first time the children had been asked to work together. The teacher did not initially tell children they could work in together, but after 5 minutes explained they could work in with the person next to them, talk about the work and read each other's. The children in this group decided to work as a group, rather than in pairs.

Excluding the fifth child, Sonia, who did not take part, all four children were active participants in this group task. Sonia did not give permission to be part of the lesson observation. The teacher suggested that she move from the group, but she wanted to stay. She said and contributed nothing but seemed to be copying the ideas that the other children were discussing, a characteristic of some children observed by Fox (2005).

Kaitlin:	((*Writing as she* speaks)) The author takes the story (5) to be finished. **Keeping to task and thinking aloud, as it is a group task.**
Zak:	So the author takes the story of the Giant's Necklace. **Adds something and displays keeping to task.**
Leon:	and they just go to Cornwall. **Adds something else, keeping to task.**
Zak:	Yeah (.) to be finished.
Kaitlin:	yet to be finished. **Improves on Zak's and keeps on task.**
Leon:	No, do that in brackets. **Makes a suggestion.**
Zak:	is yet to be finished. I'm roasting. ((*Takes off jumper*)) Yet to be finished <u>comma</u> and then to Cornwall <u>full stop</u>. **Zak does not do Leon's brackets, he uses commas**
Leon:	washed out to sea at the end. **Again Leon's comment is ignored.**
Zak:	So the author takes the story of the Giant's Necklace comma which is <u>yet</u> to be finished comma to Cornwall full stop. **Reiterates work agreed so far.**
Kaitlin:	((*Writing as she says the* words)) which is yet to be finished to Cornwall (.) Full stop? **Questions Zak's choice of punctuation.**
Zak:	Yeah 'cos there's too many commas. **Zak explains.**
Leon:	<u>in</u> Cornwall (.) You should do <u>that</u> in brackets. **Tries again for brackets.**
Kaitlin:	Why what are we doing now?
Zak:	Are you finished? (5) when she's washed out? **Refers back to Leon's earlier comment...**
Leon:	No you <u>can't</u> do that it's at the end. ... **but Leon says it can't go there.**
	~ ~ ~ ~ ~
Kaitlin:	What can we write now? **Keeping the pace of work moving on.**
Leon:	Cherry did not know there was a storm building up. **Suggestion.**
Kaitlin:	Don't put that yet.
Lydia:	that there was a storm gathering. **Makes an improvement.**
Kaitlin:	She did not know there was a storm coming in. **Gives a different version.**
Zak:	Cherry did not notice that there was a storm gathering up. **Gives another different version, not the best one, but it gets used.**
Leon:	while she was still on the beach. **Makes an improvement.**

The others all made suggestions and decisions, but Zak seems to have been the final judge of what actually was written down. Godhino and Shrimpton (2002) observed that boys often dominated discussions. However, there were times when he accepted others' views and suggestions. Kaitlin is quite dominant, suggests ideas and reaffirms what has been decided. Lydia is less dominant but made contributions at key points. Zak is the most dominant, suggests ideas, keeps the group on task, reaffirms ideas but mainly is the person who makes decisions about which suggestions are accepted. Leon is less dominant and made contributions at key points, some of which were of the highest quality. Some of his good suggestions are ignored, particularly by Zak. However, overall, the group work collaboratively and build on each others' suggestions.

It would be interesting to know what Leon and Lydia would have come up with as a pair, without the dominance of Zak and Kaitlin, as some of their suggestions that were ignored may have led to an even better piece of work. On the other hand, without Kaitlin and Zak driving the group to keep on task and contributing their ideas, perhaps Leon and Lydia might not have had their ideas.

The disagreements children had, were not evidence of disputational talk, as there was no aggression, no heated arguments and their interactions were productive. I believe it shows evidence of the early stages of exploratory talk, (Mercer, Wegerif and Dawes 1999), where students are able to disagree in a constructive way, which leads to an improved outcome. Cumulative talk would just have had them agreeing with the first suggestion offered, whereas there was evidence of children offering opinions, which they sometimes justified and explained. Jaques (2000) stresses the importance of being committed to the aims of the group and this group seem to feel valued as part of the decision making and learning process.

Other children offered different ideas but an overall decision was made and a piece of collaborative work was produced. This dialogue shows that opportunities for paired or group talk supported task completion and there was evidence of pupils scaffolding each other's learning. Children built on each other's ideas and came up with a product that was better than what they could have achieved on their own. The process of composing that end product demonstrated some skills of discussion and negotiation. Although the teacher felt these children rarely worked collaboratively, due to being a rather 'lively' group, they produced the best example of exploratory talk and the TA confirmed this lesson as better than the work they usually produced.

Key points shared by year groups

The majority of the talk observed was in the cumulative category (Mercer 2000); where the learners were co-operating, confirming one another's contributions, but not necessarily developing new ways of thinking (example Y4)

| Kelly: | It's like, you want someone to do something like save trees so you try to persuade them to do what you want. |
| Sean: | It's like when you try to make someone do something. |

There was only a little evidence of disputational talk or tension (example Y2)

Bill:	Hurry up. It's my turn after you. **Tension.**
Tom:	No it goes round in a circle. **Tension.**
Bill:	Okay. It's me after. **Tension.**
Brenda:	My turn after you. **Tension.**
Bill:	Your handwriting's small. **Tension.**

But even where certain children may exhibit some elements of competition and dominance, overall there was collaboration and co-operation. Jaques (2000) suggests that cooperation should be stressed more than competition. There was evidence that certain groups of pupils, particularly in Years 5 and 6, were beginning to show elements of exploratory talk: where they would challenge the opinion of others; justify their own viewpoint; or extend each other's contributions (example Y6)

Leon:	Cherry did not know there was a storm building up. **Suggestion.**
Kaitlin:	Don't put that yet.
Lydia:	that there was a storm gathering. **Makes an improvement.**
Kaitlin:	She did not know there was a storm coming in. **Gives a different version.**
Zak:	Cherry did not notice that there was a storm gathering up. **Gives another different version.**

(example Year 5)

Sarah:	Are you listening to this? I think that Fern should not keep the pig. **States opinion.**
David:	The Dad's a trouble maker, that's what he thinks. **Opposing view.**
Jenny:	He's not a trouble maker, the pig is too small. **Counter argument.**
Sarah:	Like a baby. **Backs up previous speaker.**
Rachel:	I'm not messing.
Julie:	Read it here, too small and could die anyway.
David:	I'm sure it says trouble maker round here.

My observations concur with Mercer, Wegerif and Dawes (1999), who conclude that exploratory talk is rare in primary classrooms. The evidence suggests that in nearly all cases, opportunities for paired or group talk supported rather than hindered task completion and that pupils scaffolded each other's learning: by offering prompts (example Year 1)

Molly:	erm what it's about is they went to get ice cream.
Jade:	((*Laughing*)) The bouncy castle and got some ice cream. **Jade builds on Molly's contribution.**

(example of prompt in Reception)

Lucy:	What comes after the dirty dirty dirty dirty mud? **Aiming for a sequence/prompt.**

through recaps (example Year 3)

Olivia:	((*Recites again*)) Be-lin-da lives in a lit-tle white house. **Gets it right.**

(example of recap in Y6)

Zak&Kaitlin:	The author takes the story of the Giant's Necklace comma which is yet to be finished comma to Cornwall full stop when a little girl named Cherry is collecting her precious pink cowry shells big enough to fit a giant. **Recap work so far.**

and by questioning (example Reception)

Lucy: What's coming next? The forest? **Asks for guidance again.**	

Although a substantial minority of children in the questionnaires responded negatively about collaborative work, the vast majority of observations showed that children were willing to share ideas with their peers and offer them support. A progression could be seen from nursery to years 5 and 6, where there was a shift from scaffolded, *reciprocal* teaching; whereby the teacher initially *models* or gives explicit demonstrations of a learning activity or skill (Palincsar and Brown 1985), to independent collaborative learning; where students know *how* to learn in cooperative learning groups (Mayer 2002, 2003). However, more training is probably needed.

Classroom Observations

These show that all classes were engaged in speaking and listening activities and offered opportunities for collaborative work. It seemed that in some classes, the children were more used to working collaboratively. This was confirmed by talking to staff, who felt they were at different stages in their confidence and familiarity with using collaborative work, as suggested by the work of Edwards (QCA 2003c) and Cameron (QCA 2003c). The children generally kept on task and completed the work given. The pattern of speaking and listening activities varied: one 15-20 minute session during a lesson; several short 1-2 minute tasks; and a combination of long and short tasks.

The shorter activities (2-5 minutes) were successful in maintaining the children's focus; enabling paired discussions about work; and offering instant and formative assessment opportunities during the lesson. The one-minute activities were often too short for children to really engage with the task, so perhaps 2 or 3 minutes would be preferable to ensure the most benefit from the activity. The longer collaborative sessions occasionally included children drifting off task, but they refocused quickly and the work was generally completed. This seemingly contradictory scenario is highlighted by Sullivan (2002) and Gustafson and MacDonald (2004). The children worked together with little conflict and most children took part. Groups tended to have one or two dominant characters that led or organised the others, but most gave opportunities for all group members to take part. A minority of children did not contribute: some copied the work of others (Fox 2005) and some preferred to work on their own and not take part in the group discussion.

Overall, the children offered ideas and suggestions for completing the tasks. Some of the work had no written outcome and was all speaking and listening; in others the written recording of work was undertaken by the pair or group, but work was often still recorded individually. Generally, the teachers explicitly told the children when they could work collaboratively, either in pairs or groups.

In summary, key issues emerging from the discourse analysis were:

- children worked collaboratively in both paired and group tasks;
- some shorter tasks lacked sufficient time for full engagement;
- children went off-task in longer activities;
- less conflict was observed in pairs;
- some exploratory talk was evident, but that talk was mainly cumulative, where children co-operated but were uncritical of contributions;
- peer talk generally supported task-completion;
- evidence existed of peer scaffolding;
- despite some negativity, most children preferred collaborative work.

Chapter Six: Reflections on the Research Process, Conclusions and Recommendations

Reflections: Effectiveness of research process, data and findings.

Classroom observations were undertaken from Nursery to Y6 (7 lessons in total, resulting in 22 different dialogues). As anticipated, it was difficult to remain a non-participant observer: as the children were very keen to involve me in their work. Evidence that this did not skew my findings can be seen in the transcripts; they soon ignored the microphone and got on with their work. It was difficult moving around the room trying to record different groups of children, but I soon got used to setting up very quickly. It was hard to make research notes in my journal, as I had to keep brief field notes of what the children were doing but also have a system to show which child was speaking, so I could identify them for later transcriptions. I wrote a quick table plan and numbered the children, jotting the first and last few words each said in a conversation. This helped transcribing, as although I could usually distinguish between voices, I would not have been able to determine which child was speaking, without my coded field notes. The children had asked to choose their made-up names for my transcripts, so these were written alongside the numbered table plan.

Transcribing was a time-consuming task, particularly as the equipment I was using did not allow me to download the dialogues onto the computer to use software packages to aid transcription (budget constraints). Even though the microphone had been carefully selected as one with a limited range and direction, designed to tape the immediate children, there was still a lot of background noise.

I spoke to groups of children about their attitudes to collaborative work and speaking and listening activities. A mobile classroom was used, to minimise background noise. This was helpful but the children were excitable and tended to all talk at once initially. It became clear that ground rules needed setting, to ensure the process went more smoothly, such as having a signal from me to denote who could answer. There was a mixture of open and closed questions. The difficulty with the Nursery and Reception children was that they were reluctant to talk, or wanted to talk about other things around them. Many children expressed surprise that I should want to ask their opinions, as well as that of their teachers.

The after-school staff interviews were much easier to record and transcribe, as there was mainly one person talking. Although some nerves were admitted to, the information seemed to flow quite naturally. In hindsight perhaps my questions were too structured and there should have been more opportunity for open comments, but staff seemed at ease enough to express their views.

Modifications:

If I were to undertake this type of research again, there are changes and improvements I would make, due to certain issues that arose during the research.

- Interview TAs as a group, as a potential contrast from teacher and child attitudes.
- Add in a question asking children if they feel work has to involve reading or writing or whether they consider speaking and listening as work.
- Reconsider many of children's interview questions, as some overlap or are too similar.
- Alter some of the teachers' interview questions, as some are too structured. Although I intended to use semi-structured interviews, the majority of the interview time was based around a set of questions the staff had in advance.
- Interview Head, although we had many informal conversations.
- Interview SEN Teacher, although we had spoken previously.
- Do recording in quieter areas: A couple of class/group observation were recorded outside the classroom, where children work in a 'quiet' area. This was much easier when it came to transcriptions, as there was less background noise. However, to do it like this all the time may not accurately represent classroom reality.
- Examine gender variations in attitudes towards peer collaboration, speaking and listening, by asking children to specify boy or girl on children's questionnaire.
- Reduce size of children's interview groups: Groups of 8 children too big to be easily managed, 4 children would probably have been enough. The group size did at times present some management problems: turn taking and in some cases behaviour.
- Examine samples of marked work, as it was difficult to assess task completion (as I did not collect their work in at the end and did not usually have the chance to find out from the teacher whether their work was better or worse than usual). I only had

my impressions to use of whether work was successful and I did not know the children well enough to judge this.

- Set ground rules for children's groups, to improve children's interaction.
- Need more expensive directional microphone, as background noise made it hard to transcribe.
- Request documentation before study commences. I asked to collect the documentation relating to speaking and listening and collaborative work: such as literacy plans; excerpts from Ofsted reports and Action Plans; school policies; training courses or INSET attended; class lists. This aspect is incomplete, as I did not receive the documentation during the research period, because the Head and Literacy Co-ordinator each thought that the other one was gathering the information. The documentation was due to be posted on, but was never received.
- Clarify how much information to present to school, as staff had different ideas about the level of detail they would like to see in their report, from a brief overview to the whole research project.

However, on balance, the data collected allowed me to meet my overall research aim. The only data lacking, which would have helped provide an extra way of triangulating findings, was the School Documentation, most of which was not made available. Due to the limited amount of data, it is not possible to fully comment on this. There was ample data from teacher and pupil questionnaires and interviews to highlight teacher and pupil attitudes to speaking and listening; paired and groups talk; and peer collaboration. The interviews did provide some supplementary evidence to support the questionnaires. There were four types of data (children's and teachers' questionnaires and interviews) for just one learning objective (teacher and pupil attitudes to collaborative work). In contrast, the discourse analyses, although one form of data, allowed me to evaluate three of my objectives. Observations, as a method of collecting data, fed into all research objectives, but specifically revealed the opportunities for collaborative work. The one data type I would have collected in hindsight is a breakdown of gender on children's questionnaires. Overall, the data collection methods were appropriate for obtaining the findings that would meet the aim of my research.

Summary relating findings to research objectives

- **To identify the opportunities that pupils have to work collaboratively through talk** ~ a range of short and long activities were observed, covering all classes, including paired and group work. The short activities sometimes lacked sufficient time for pupils to think, reflect and engage in the task. At times, the children went off task in longer activities. Children appeared to work more co-operatively in pairs rather than in groups.

- **To analyse the types and quality of talk** ~ there was some evidence of disputational talk, where competition, dominant characters and arguments prevented or hindered the completion of work. The quality of talk was mainly cumulative, where children co-operated, but were uncritical of each other's contributions. Tasks were completed, but perhaps a more advanced level of work may have been achieved with more discussion and negotiation. There was some evidence of early exploratory talk in Y5 and Y6, where children questioned, challenged and justified different opinions, to try and achieve the best result. However, in some group activities, paired work may have been more efficient.

- **To investigate whether opportunities for paired or group talk support or hinder task completion** ~ the evidence suggests that group work was not generally a hindrance to task completion. Although some children lacked the necessary skills to work effectively in groups, the observations did show some evidence of co-operation and mutual support. For some children, it might have been the case that they may have completed tasks more effectively on their own. Paired work did seem to support children's learning and did not have the problem of distractions that were sometimes found in group work.

- **To look for evidence of pupils scaffolding each other's learning** ~ there was evidence of children supporting each other to move learning forward, by giving each other prompts; recapping on work done; keeping each other on task; sharing ideas and strategies; asking questions.

- **To explore pupils' and teachers' attitudes to paired and group talk** ~ although a substantial minority of children did not value collaborative work, there was a high level of support and enthusiasm from staff and children for peer talk and how it supports learning. There were issues from both staff and pupils about the management of group work and a need was felt for further training in how to promote effective collaborative work.

Aim: To investigate the relationship between peer talk, collaborative work and learning ~ the evidence suggests that collaborative work can move pupils' learning forward and that effective oral skills, including the ability to work effectively in groups, is needed to maximise the potential learning. However, findings also suggest that an area of development to focus on is how to move from Mercer's cumulative talk to exploratory talk. Groups working with minimal input or teacher guidance may only be able operate at a limited quality of talk and cooperation. From the data available it seems that children may need more initial support in developing the skills to scaffold each other's learning and of higher levels of negotiation and critical discussion.

Conclusions and Recommendations

The evidence from teacher and children's interviews and questionnaires in chapter 4, illustrates there is a high level of support for collaborative work to support learning (Harmon 2002) and for speaking and listening. However, this evidence also shows a substantial minority of children feeling unhappy about peer work: the replies giving reasons of disruption, noise and copying (Fox 2005). It can be useful to establish some rules for talk, to prevent potential chaos (Mercer 2000). The negativity towards peer work could indicate that the status of collaborative work needs increasing, by raising the profile of speaking and listening within the school. It is important to emphasise to children and parents that talking is still work and as important as reading and writing (Czerniewska 1992). This could be achieved by ensuring children know they are specifically being assessed in speaking and listening; focussing school reward systems to include speaking and listening work, not just for reading and writing; having particular projects in each year group, such as presentations, designing radio/TV programmes, having a debate, a drama production. However, the transcripts do show that children did scaffold and support each other's learning to some extent (Gustafson and MacDonald 2004). This needs celebrating and publicising, so both staff and pupils can discuss successes.

The tables in chapter 4 (pp. 46-48), showing the perceived amounts of time engaged in paired and group work, indicate differences between teacher and pupil perceptions. The staff believe that more collaborative work is taking place than do children. This may indicate a need to specify speaking, listening and collaborative work on planning, to focus attention on this area. Unfortunately, much of the documentation requested was not given. However, the interview responses indicate that planning tends to be confined to reading and writing activities, with some staff annotating 'sp and l' to denote oral work. This is arguably not enough to ensure that sufficient oral work is taking place, particularly when the National Curriculum has speaking and listening as one third of the English requirements.

The discourse analyses indicate that all lessons included opportunities to work collaboratively and that there were differences in the amount of paired and group work. Although there was evidence of paired and group work in all lessons, the exchanges did not always maximise learning potential. It is important for teachers to show children how to work together effectively (Gibbs 1994). The transcript analyses in chapter 5 show, for example, that some of the tasks were too short to be effective. The paired activities need to be longer, in order for the children to have time to think and discuss the task. Paired activities should be part of the whole class sessions, as it gives children more time to think before having to answer or feedback to the class. It is also effective when the children go back to their tables after the teacher input. However, the key issue is training the children in the features of exploratory talk and therefore modelling how to work effectively in groups. The younger children may benefit from more paired work before group work is introduced. Children need to have a shared understanding of what constitutes collaborative work and a structure or teacher guidance on effective ways of working, thinking and talking (Corden 2000).

The table in chapter 4, p38, highlights that although there were more paired activities, the actual time spend on group work was higher. The transcript analyses show that longer paired activities often produced better work and less conflict, so perhaps the school could consider this when planning (Fox 2005). Also, to improve the quality of group work and interaction, some modelling and training in collaborative work could be a focus for teaching (Sullivan, 2002). There needs to be an improvement in the quality of talk, to move learning forward, by modelling the language children need, in order to negotiate and explore ideas. (Rojas-Drummond 2000 and Mattos 2000).

Group work needs structuring so children are clear about their responsibilities and roles in completing tasks (Godhino and Shrimpton 2002) and feel part of the learning and decision making process (Jaques 2000). These group tasks do not have to be confined to literacy lessons. Teachers need to model and demonstrate appropriate language and behaviour while initially being a group member; and then move towards only intervening when necessary; and finally withdrawing as the children become more competent. It is crucial to be careful not to withdraw support and scaffolding before the children are ready (Brown and Palincsar 1985).

The discourse analyses in chapter 5 show that the quality of talk was mainly of a cumulative nature (Mercer 2000), with the beginnings of exploratory talk in years 5 and 6 (Mercer, Wegerif and Dawes1999). This indicates there are further opportunities to move children's learning forward, by modelling the type of talk and questioning needed to promote higher order thinking skills. I saw evidence of some modelling of language in the early years, as detailed in the Nursery transcript analysis in chapter 5. Modelling language, therefore, might be an area the school could focus on, such as encouraging children by using open-ended questions and supplementary questions to extend discussions (Wray and Lewis 2005). Observations in Year 1, as shown in the transcript analysis in chapter 5, seem to show that modelling has taken place: the children are clearly used to working in pairs. The emphasis placed on speaking and listening in Year 5, evidenced from the observations and the staff interview, seem to show that this has helped to produce the early stages of exploratory talk observed in Y5 and Y6 lessons. This type of work could be extended and where there are still difficulties and concerns over class management (Edwards QCA 2003c), as seen in the staff questionnaires and children's interviews, the make up of the groups could be more carefully considered.

The staff questionnaires, in chapter 4, highlight a strong need for further training on talk as a tool for learning and perhaps this could be one starting point when planning for staff development on increasing peer work (Cameron in QCA 2003c). The interviews showed that staff had only managed to have a brief and recent glimpse at the Primary Strategy materials for speaking and listening, so here is an area in which staff can support themselves, as the materials exist for promoting oracy. Staff feedback also showed a variation in confidence in delivering effective oracy teaching, so perhaps team teaching, using more confident and experienced staff, could be a way forward.

Overall, the school had many strengths to build on, as there is a high level of commitment to oracy; evidence of a range of paired and group activities; and the early stages of effective modelling for quality speaking and listening skills. The recommended main points for action are: to use the speaking and listening materials; plan specifically for oracy; raise the status of speaking and listening; increase the length of paired activities; implement effective oracy assessment and receive staff training in how to promote effective group work skills.

It is important to also examine my findings in a context beyond the school that was the focus of this study, as there are wider implications. Although case study findings in one school cannot necessarily be extrapolated to apply to all schools, it can be suggested that a similar range of attitudes would be found among other schools' staff and children. Likewise, a range of teacher-led and children's peer group work may be observed in other schools. Research of the literature suggests that better oracy and an increased skill in collaborative work leads to peer scaffolding, exploratory talk and increased thinking and learning. The research and findings in this case study tend to follow the wider research. Therefore, improved language and co-operation may be seen to lead to higher levels of learning. It seems that there is some evidence of collaboration supporting learning and that with a greater status given to speaking and listening and an increased emphasis and modelling of oracy, it would ensure children would benefit from peer work. This has implications for the staff development of existing teachers and support staff in all schools, but also for the training of new teachers.

This small study indicates that more training is needed for current practitioners and suggests that it may be also be a key issue in initial teacher training. A focus is needed on how to teach speaking and listening effectively and how to foster the skills of group work. I have already altered the English modules in the ITT programmes to reflect a greater emphasis on teaching oracy and collaborative work. I have used selected transcripts for students to analyse talk, in terms of Mercer's categories of cumulative, disputational and exploratory talk. Students work in pairs to analyse children's talk and then peer review each other's discourse analysis of the transcripts. Only a small sample of transcripts was used and then students were given my analysis to compare with theirs. I have also use the transcripts for students to assess the role of collaborative work in promoting children's learning and to identify interventions that could have been made to support learning. Students will also have a school-based task to observe group work in school and to evaluate the skills children have to work collaboratively. There will be a focus on analysing and then formulating interventions to increase the quality of talk and improve collaborative skills. Pairs of students also plan and teach a speaking and listening activity to a group of children, evaluating its success.

In my current post I have observed that many teacher training students need support with their own oral communication and team working skills. So, in addition to increasing oracy in English ITT provision, I am planning to undertake further research on students' oral skills and particularly the dynamics of working in teams. This should yield data not only to support students working collaboratively but also demonstrate practically to them how they can use these skills in the classroom to develop children's exploratory talk, peer scaffolding and collaborative skills.

~   ~   ~   ~   ~

Appendices

A   **School Correspondence**
             Not included, as confidential.

B   **School Proformas (blank)**   **p90**
B1   Staff Questionnaire
B2   Children's Questionnaire
B3   Teacher Interview Questions
B4   Children's Group Interview Questions

C   **Methodology**   **p96**
C1   Methodology summary

D   **Transcripts**   **p97**
D1   Class Observations (7)
D2   Teacher Interviews (4)
D3   Children's Group Interviews (4)
D4   Open Questions from Staff Questionnaire

E   **Charts, Tables and Other Data**   **p158**
E1   How Children Prefer To Work (by year group)
E2   Results from Teacher and Support Staff Questionnaire,
             with separate figures for teaching and support staff.

Bibliography   **p163**

B1 Staff Questionnaire

Staff Questionnaire				
I would appreciate your help by completing this questionnaire: Please √ boxes				
Teacher ☐ TA/NNEB/Support Staff ☐ Other ☐				

	Please complete both sides of questionnaire – Thank you!	Agree strongly	Agree	Disagree	Disagree strongly
1	Speaking and listening are just as important as reading and writing.				
2	Speaking and listening are vital to promote reading and writing.				
3	Speaking and listening activities are difficult to manage.				
4	Children enjoy speaking and listening activities.				
5	Children prefer to work in pairs or groups, rather than on their own.				
6	I would prefer children to work independently.				
7	Children mess about during speaking and listening activities.				
8	Children benefit from working collaboratively with their peers.				
9	Children complete tasks better when they work with others.				
10	I have seen children supporting each others' learning.				
11	I have received enough training for promoting speaking and listening.				
12	I would like to receive more training for promoting speaking and listening.				
13	I have a range of resources for promoting speaking and listening.				
14	I plan specifically for speaking and listening activities.				
15	I only teach speaking and listening in literacy.				
16	I teach speaking and listening in many curricular subjects.				
17	I encourage the children to work in pairs.				
18	I encourage the children to work in groups.				
19	Children still record their work individually even if they do a task in groups.				
20	I find speaking and listening difficult to assess.				

		Every lesson	Every day	2 or 3 times a week	Once a week	Less than weekly
21	How often do you allow children to work in pairs?					
22	How often do you allow children to work in groups?					

23	What are the positive and negative aspects of speaking and listening, for the teacher and for the children?

24	What are the benefits and disadvantages of children working collaboratively, for the teacher and for the children?

Please use the space below for any other comments.

Thank you for completing this questionnaire ~ **Beth**

B2 Children's Questionnaire

You do not need to write your name, but please write your year group here:-   Year___

How do you prefer to work in class, most of the time?

Please choose only one of these and tick its box:

1.	On my own.	
2.	In a pair (with one friend).	
3.	In a group.	

Please write the reason for your choice, either below or on the other side of this paper. Thank you!

....

You do not need to write your name, but please write your year group here:-   Year___

How do you prefer to work in class, most of the time?

Please choose only one of these and tick its box:

1.	On my own.	
2.	In a pair (with one friend).	
3.	In a group.	

Please write the reason for your choice, either below or on the other side of this paper. Thank you!

B3 Teacher Interview Questions

Foundation	KS1	Lower KS2	Upper KS2	
				Comments
1	Do you think speaking and listening receives less emphasis than reading and writing, and if so, why?			
2	In your opinion, are there any factors to do with the school or local area that affect children's speaking and listening skills?			
3	What do you think of the recent box of materials to support speaking and listening?			
4	Do you have any concerns about the planning, teaching and assessment of speaking and listening and also children working together?			
5	Do you specifically tell children when they can work together and does this vary according to the lesson?			
6	In your opinion, does collaborative work support or hinder task completion?			
7	Do you think that children can support each other's learning, and if so, in what ways?			
8	Do you feel that children complete their work better when working independently?			
9	What would be the most effective means in developing your skills in planning, teaching and assessing speaking and listening and also promoting collaborative work?			
10	How do you plan for speaking and listening activities?			
11	How do you organise and teach speaking and listening activities?			

12	How do you assess speaking and listening activities?	
13	What benefits do you believe can come from collaborative work? a) For the staff. b) For the children.	
14	Do you feel under pressure that every child should record something every lesson?	
15	In what ways do you model speaking and listening? (Compared with how you would in shared reading and shared writing).	
16	How do you foster and promote paired and group work?	
17	What types of speaking and listening activities do you use in different curricular areas?	
18	Do you think the Foundation Stage Curriculum and the NLS give enough objectives and support to plan, teach and assess speaking and listening?	
19	Do you think that the year group children are in makes speaking and listening or collaborative work any more important or difficult to teach?	
20	Do you have any comments that you would like to add about speaking and listening or children working collaboratively?	

Any supplementary questions used and general comments

B4 Children's Interviews

Children's Interviews						
Age group:	Foundation	KS1		Lower KS2		Upper KS2
		Every lesson	Every day	2 or 3 times a week	Once a week	Less than weekly
1	How often do you work on your own?					
2	How often do you work in pairs?					
3	How often do you work in groups?					
4	What kind of speaking and listening activities have you done?					
5	What do you like about speaking and listening activities?					
6	Is there anything you dislike about speaking and listening activities?					
7	Which do you prefer, reading, writing or speaking and listening?					
8	Is it more difficult to work on your own than working with a friend?					
9	What are the things you like or dislike about working on your own?					
10	What is good or bad about working with other children?					
11	How can you help your friends in class?					
12	How can your friends help you in class?					
13	If you are stuck with your work, who do you ask? Teacher/ friend/ or both?					
14	When people are talking, how can you show you are listening?					
15	What can you do to make sure working together goes well?					
Any supplementary questions used and general comments:						

C1 Methodology

Title and Aim of Project:

An investigation into the opportunities for peer group talk in the classroom.

Objectives:

- To identify the opportunities that pupils have to work collaboratively through talk.
- To analyse the types and quality of talk.
- To investigate whether opportunities for paired or group talk support or hinder task completion.
- To look for evidence of pupils scaffolding each other's learning.
- To explore pupils' and teachers' attitudes to paired and group talk.

Methodology:

* Questionnaire (all staff).

* Interview (4 staff: ~ one each from Foundation, KS1, lower KS2 and upper KS2, including the Literacy Co-ordinator).

* Record children's conversations with each other in a literacy lesson, from Nursery to Y6 (8 x 1 hour lessons).

* Ask children to state a preference for how they prefer to work and give reasons why. (Staff would be willing to do this within their classes, I would support the younger children who will need their reasons scribing).
      (1) I prefer to work alone.
      (2) I prefer to work in pairs.
      (3) I prefer to work in groups.

* Speak to groups of children (4-8 at a time, equal mix of gender) about their attitudes to speaking and listening activities.
      ~ Foundation
      ~ KS1
      ~ Lower KS2
      ~ Upper KS2

* Collect documentation relating to speaking and listening and collaborative work: such as literacy plans; excerpts from Ofsted reports and Action Plans; school policies; training courses or INSET attended; class lists (so I can alter names).

Year N (morning group) Friday June 11th – Lesson based on a garage role play.

Task One (Track 21) 20 minutes

Simon	Owen	Giles	Matthew	Fred	Susan

Background information – teacher introducing a new role play area, spent 30 minutes as a whole class suggesting vocabulary relating to garages, building on previous day when teacher had shown the children around her car. As it was a new role play, the teacher prompted by modelling appropriate vocabulary, sentences and phrases, but the children were still interacting with each other, so the session has been considered as peer talk and therefore transcribed. It took place in the playground and the actual garage was an under cover extension to the classroom.

Susan:	It's wet. ((*The car*))
Teacher:	<OH NO> we'll have to get the towel to dry it.
Susan:	THE RAIN'S BEEN POURING ON IT. **Comes up with her own vocabulary.**
Teacher:	Ah.
	((*Screaming*))
Simon:	It's been raining on it. **Copies Susan**
Teacher:	Who is going to be the car drivers? **Intervenes to get role play underway**
Susan:	[ME.
Giles:	ME.
Owen:	ME]
Teacher:	You two go and get in the cars ((*Giles and Owen*))
Susan:	((*Gets in to the police car*))
Teacher:	Do <u>you</u> want to be a mechanic then? ((*To Simon, Matthew and Fred*)) So you are going to be a police lady are you Susan? **Suggests roles.**
Susan:	Yeah. I'm off.
Teacher:	Put your feet in first ((*To Owen*))
Simon:	Oil tch tch tch (*Making noises for squirting oil into a car*)) **Shows he has ideas about appropriate behaviour.**
Giles:	I want the blue car.
Teacher:	You'll have to have the red one.
Matthew:	Two blue mechanics. **Short utterance.**
	((*Two children 'driving' around the 'road,' one in the garage*))
Teacher:	The police car is in to be repaired. You can fix the police car and put the tool box and the cones in the back of the breakdown truck.
Owen:	Can two go in Miss or one?
Teacher:	Only one, this is going to be mended inside.
Susan:	There's something dead on the floor.
Teacher:	There's something <u>dead</u> on the floor.
Fred:	I found a lighter. ((*Picking it up off the playground*))
Teacher:	Don't touch that it is dangerous ((*Child had picked it up and thrown it through the school railings*)) Right cars <stop> Someone is going to have to break down and someone is going to have to come for petrol. Fred, Fred can you come and fix this motor car please. Come on, you get your tools out and see what's the matter with this.
Fred:	I need the <tools>. **Short utterance, takes cue from teacher.**
Susan:	I'm on the road. **Short utterance, related to role play, but unclear if to Fred.**
Teacher:	Tell Fred what to do to this car and then you can write down what's wrong with it.
Susan:	It's broken. **Short utterance, related to role play.**
Matthew:	((*With clipboard*)) It's broken. I want a pen to write it down with. **Becomes involved and says more than the others' short utterances.**
	((*Owen, Susan and Giles are all now driving around*))
Giles:	((*Breaks down*))
Susan&Owen:	((*Go for petrol*))
Matthew:	I need a hammer.

Owen:	My petrol cap is this way.
Fred:	((*Hammers Giles' car*))
Simon:	((*Pretends to put oil in Susan's car*))
	Last few lines show all children involved in role play, but in pairs: Matthew/Owen, Fred/Giles, Simon/Susan.
Teacher:	Right Matthew, you've got a customer for petrol. **Teacher intervenes to move activity and language forward.**
Owen:	I need petrol. **Takes cue from teacher.**
Matthew:	How much petrol do you want? **Responds to Owen.**
Owen:	How much money?
	((*Constant hammering noises by Fred on Giles' car*))
Teacher:	You have to pay for it. Ask the petrol pump attendant how much he is going to charge you, ask how much you owe him.
Owen:	((*Pretends to pay*))
Teacher:	Is it one pound or one penny?
Giles:	Miss is that the oil one? (10) My car wants to go home.
Matthew:	Hello what do you want? ((*To Susan*))
Susan:	Petrol.
Matthew:	((*Matthew put petrol nozzle in car*)) It's filled up.
Teacher:	What do you say to the petrol pump attendant? **Prompts.**
Susan:	THANK YOU **Responds to prompt.**
Fred:	((*Pretending to put oil in*)) There's all our spare wheels.
Giles:	My car needs a wheel. **Interacting with Fred.**
Matthew:	((*Writes number of car on clipboard*)) I can't write his name down 'cos it's too hard. **Again, Matthew uses longer sentences than the others.**
	((*Susan, Simon (who had been a mechanic) and Owen now driving around*))
Simon:	((*Drives into garage*)) I need petrol.
Fred:	((*Puts petrol in*)) ALL DONE.
Susan:	Go to the garage. ((*To Owen*))
Owen:	((*Obeys and comes to garage*))
Teacher:	I think you should tell him to write it in and write your name down. What is wrong with it? Has it got a broken engine or does it need a new wheel? You need to get a spanner and pliers. **Scaffolds.**
Fred:	((*Pretends to jack up the car*)) ZZZZZZZZZZZZZZZ **Responds.**
Owen:	The wheel's broke. **Responds.**
Fred:	I've took the wheel off it needs two new tyres. **Interacts with Owen, using longer sentences.**
Teacher:	Two new tyres (.) that's going to be expensive.
Matthew:	Are you going to write his name down? **Again, uses a longer sentence.**
Giles:	My car's broke. **Short utterance.**
Teacher:	Can you fix it straight away or does he have to come back later? The garage looks a bit full. **Models vocabulary and longer sentences.**
Fred:	Do you want me to fix that? I can do it now or bring it back later. **Responds to teacher's modelled language, by using similar words and longer sentences.**
Matthew:	Do it in a minute.
Teacher:	Have you put the wheel back on? Is it ready to drive away now?
Fred:	I took the wheel off I took the wheel off (30) You can go.
Teacher:	Have you taken his money?
Fred:	Oh yeah
Teacher:	Give him a receipt to show the work is done. Have a nice day.
Susan:	((*Susan drives in*)) My car's broke. My car's broke. Can you do it now?
Fred:	What's wrong?
Teacher:	The garage is too full, ask this lady ((*points to Susan*)) to sit in reception and wait until her car is fixed.
Fred:	Do you want to sit in the reception? **Responds to teacher prompt, by using similar language.**
Teacher:	Maybe you can ask her to write her name down. **More prompts.**
Susan:	((*Sits down on the chair in 'reception'*))
Fred:	I need to put the screw in ((*Hammering*))
Matthew:	I'll hammer it in and you screw it. **Responding to Fred.**
Teacher:	Where's the other tool box gone?

Matthew:	((*Hammering furiously*)) Oh. Too windy (10) Your car's fixed.
Teacher:	((*To Susan*)) Well it looks alright to me, maybe he's coming round with it now.
Fred:	YOUR CAR'S FIXED.
Teacher:	Is she going to have to have a receipt? A receipt for the money.
Matthew:	It's too windy for me.
Susan:	NO
Teacher:	I think it's nearly time to close the garage up.
Susan:	I'll get the car.
Matthew:	That's 20 ½ ((*Measuring car*)) That <u>is</u> 20 ½
Fred:	That's your receipt ((*To Susan*)) (10) Has your car broken down? ((*Running out at Simon*))
Teacher:	Fred. I'm sure the mechanic doesn't run out in the street, wait until somebody comes into the garage. **Suggesting appropriate behaviour.**
Susan:	((*Gets back in car*))
Teacher:	We're not fixing that one today, we're going to fix that tomorrow. What time does he have to come back tomorrow to pick up his car?
Fred:	Friday.
Teacher:	Yes but what time?
Fred:	Half past 5. ((*Children go and 'park' the cars in the 'car park' and leave one in the 'garage' to be 'repaired'*))

It is clear that Fred has responded to the teacher's prompt by using vocabulary modelled by the teacher, forming longer sentences. Other suggestions from the teacher included:

Teacher:	Tell Fred what to do to this car and then you can write down what's wrong with it.
Teacher:	You have to pay for it. Ask the petrol pump attendant how much he is going to charge you, ask how much you owe him.
Teacher:	The garage is too full, ask this lady ((*points to Susan*)) to sit in reception and wait until her car is fixed.

There are times when children speak in longer sentences, but these are rare. Examples:

Susan: THE RAIN'S BEEN POURING ON IT.

Matthew: ((*With clipboard*)) It's broken. I want a pen to write it down with.

It is interesting to note, however, that they often worked as a pair – perhaps because at their stage of development, this is easier to cope with.

Year R Wednesday June 9th – Lesson based on *We're Going on a Bear Hunt.*

Looking at story maps to remind about the sequence of the story. Asked during shared time to 'think of a nice sentence for each part of the story' and 'you can chat to a friend about the sentence but you don't have to if you don't want to'. A couple of children whispered but it was too quiet to hear, most were silent, so the teacher asked for contributions. This did not allow the children enough time to discuss a sentence with a partner. Individuals gave suggestions and the teacher scribed the sentences. This was a missed opportunity to have the children working in pairs.

Task (Track 11) 20 minutes
| Jane | Ruby | Lucy | Helen | Alice |

During group and independent time, after whole class session. Teacher explicitly told children to talk about work to each other. This group had to make story characters out of play dough, place on the story map and retell the story together.

Alice:	The Dad.
Jane:	The grass.
Lucy:	Everything is squashy. **'Squashy' as in the book.**

Jane:	Squashy. **Repeats Lucy.**
Lucy:	I'm making I'm making grass.
Helen:	((*Singing*)) I'm making grass. **Repeats Lucy.**
Jane:	It looks like a chicken. I'll make grass again.
Lucy:	I made the grass. **Assumes task is complete.**
Jane:	I'm making the grass too long. **Following earlier comment.**
Ruby:	The grass is too big. **1st contribution.**
Jane:	It's grass, squishy squashy. **Repeats Lucy's earlier comment.**
Helen:	I'm doing clean grass.
Jane:	I'm making the grass hot. Make your grass hot.
Ruby:	I've already made my grass hot.
Jane:	A little tiny grass.
Lucy:	That's not the grass.
Jane:	Look at my grass Lucy.
Ruby:	Mine's too big. **Said this earlier.**
Helen:	((*Singing again*)) River river river river. **'River' also in book.**
Alice:	I've finished my grass. What's after that?
Lucy:	I'm doing so many.
Jane:	I'm making mine I'll make my forest.
Helen:	My grass.
Lucy:	Oozy mud. **Again, appropriate vocabulary from the book.**
Ruby:	Lucy you've done it in the wrong space ((*Laughing*)) It's upside down.
Lucy:	Now I'm gonna put (.) river's coming next.
Jane:	It looks like seaweed this green thing ((*Pointing at the green play dough*)).
Lucy:	I'm making the water. This is the water.
Alice:	This is my river it's hard to get the river down ((*Laughing*))
Jane:	Need more.
Ruby:	I only need 4 more.
Alice:	It's the forest.
Helen:	I'm making my water <u>dirty.</u>
Alice:	Dirty water.
Jane:	I'm making mine clean water.
Ruby:	How come it's got to be clean?
Jane:	We've got to tell the story again. **So far, only key words mentioned.**
Lucy:	I've done the water.
Helen:	Lucy you forgot one piece.
Jane:	Silly silly sausage.
Ruby:	Silly silly sausage.
Lucy:	What's coming next? The forest?
Ruby:	I'm doing the forest.
Helen:	I'm doing the forest.
Alice:	I've done my forest. **No collaboration, all doing their own work.**
Jane:	I only need 2 more now.
Ruby:	You haven't done your water. **Prompted, is this scaffolding?**
Lucy:	That's the water.
Alice:	The snowstorm.
Ruby:	Is that yours?
Helen:	I'm making the mud dirty dirty dirty.
Jane:	Look at all my dirty mud.
Lucy:	What comes after the dirty dirty dirty dirty mud? **Aiming for a sequence/prompt.**
Helen:	A snowstorm. Mine's squishy.
Lucy:	Where's the snowstorm?
Alice:	It's all the little dots.
Lucy:	Little dots.
Alice:	I'm gonna do a bear. **All these elements are in the book but they are not re-telling the story in sequence.**
Lucy:	What comes after the snowstorm? **Trying to get work done, seeks help – peer scaffolding perhaps.**
Jane:	The forest.
Lucy:	I'm almost finished now.
Helen:	Mine's nearly finished.

Ruby:	Mine's not.
Alice:	Mine is.
Helen:	Mine's squishy.
Ruby:	Mine's squishy squashy.
Helen:	((*Singing*)) Squishy squashy squishy squishy.
Lucy:	I'm finished.
Jane:	I'm not.
Ruby:	I are.
Helen:	Finished.
Alice:	Finished.
Jane:	I stick all mine on.
Lucy:	Press the mud hard.
Jane:	I've nearly finished.
Lucy:	Press the mud on hard.
Jane:	Ooh. ((*Pressing 'mud' down*))
Alice:	Let's tell the story now. **At last, someone remembers the task.**
Jane:	Let everybody finish first.
Lucy:	We've already finished.
Ruby:	Ha ha I beat Jane.
Helen:	No you haven't, you haven't done the water.
Ruby:	My water's gonna be white.
Lucy:	Water can't be white can they?
Alice:	It can be any colour.
Lucy:	They've gotta be blue, haven't they?
Ruby:	It can be blue or white.
Helen:	It'll have to be green and white.
Lucy:	Put some on.
Alice:	She doesn't want to.
Lucy:	You have to Ruby.
Helen:	You have to like ours.
Jane:	Push it down. ((*Flattens the play dough*))
Helen:	The cave is going smaller smaller. I'm pressing it too hard. ((*She has covered up the cave entrance with play dough*))
Jane:	I forgot what my story is.
Helen:	I've done my cave ((*Chanting*)) I've done my cave
Ruby:	You've covered the way in.
	((*Alice has everything neat, the others have just flattened play dough on everything*))
Lucy:	You have to cover the way in haven't we?
Helen:	How are they going to get in?
Lucy:	I've done a space so they can get in.
Jane:	They're all lost.
Lucy:	No they're not all lost.
Alice:	They don't want to see the bear in there.
Ruby:	In out in out.
Lucy:	They have to stick it in before the bear comes out. They don't want to see the bear.
Helen:	They don't want to see the bear. They don't want to see the bear. They don't want to see the bear.
Alice:	I like bears anyway.
Jane:	I do.
Lucy:	They don't want to see the bear. They don't want to see the bear.
Helen:	I like bears.
Alice:	If everybody's done it you've got to tell the story now. **Task reminder again from Alice.**
Lucy:	Okay. That's better. ((*She takes play dough off cave entrance*)).
Helen:	We've got to start.
Lucy:	Who's gonna start first?
Jane:	Where did they go down?
Lucy:	Tell the story. Tell it or I'll tell it by myself. Okay. They went through the grass first (.) and then they went through the water.
Ruby:	Lucy Lucy
Jane:	Everybody can tell the story.

Lucy:	They went through the woods.
Helen:	Put your hand up if you want to tell the story cos they're all shy.
Lucy:	You want to tell the story.
Ruby:	Put your hand up in the middle if you don't want to tell the story.
Lucy:	Who's gonna start?
Jane:	Not me.
Helen:	You start.
Ruby:	Okay okay okay okay.
Lucy:	Start the story.
Alice:	Everyone's gone shy.
Jane:	Okay okay I'm not shy I'll tell the story. First we went to the grass and then we went to the (unclear) and then we went to the water and then they went to the…
Ruby:	Splishy splashy
Helen:	The grass went swishy swashy.
Jane:	You've got to say the sounds.
Alice:	You can't just say they went they went.
Lucy:	They went in the forest. I didn't listen. Splish splash, swishy swashy.
Helen:	Put your hands in the middle to tell the story.
Alice:	I'll tell the grass, you'll tell the water.
Jane:	I'll tell the water.
Ruby:	I'm telling the cave.
Lucy:	Squelch squirch.
Helen:	I'm telling the last one.

Teacher calls them back for plenary and each group feeds back on their activity.
During group and independent work time, after the whole class input session, the teacher explicitly told the children to talk about work to each other.

Year 1 Thursday June 10th – Lesson based on recounts.

Task One (Track 16) 10 minutes
Carl   Rob

Teacher explicitly told children to work in pairs for their phonics (phonemes frame), to take turns to scribe on white board. Teacher gave a clear explanation of how to work together and why this was beneficial for the children (talk to each other and decide what to write).

Teacher:	First word is an easy one, it's man, <u>man</u>.
Carl:	'm' you want an 'm' **Offers suggestion**.
Rob:	((*Writes 'm' Carl watches*)) **Rob in the scribe for the 1st word.**
Carl:	'a' **Offers the next letter.**
Rob:	((*Writes 'a'*)) **Scribes.**
Carl:	That's a 'n' **Suggests final letter.**
Rob:	'm' ((*Writes 'm'*)) **Makes a mistake.**
Carl:	'<u>n</u>' at the end. **Peer scaffolding.**
Rob:	YES
Carl:	Ready ready ready.
Rob:	No.
Teacher:	The next word is shed. (3) <u>Shed.</u>
Carl:	<u>Shed.</u> ((*Tries to sound it out*)) S-e-d. Shed. Sh-e-d. **Has a try.**
Rob:	It's got 'e' **Makes a suggestion.**
Carl:	What about 'sh'?
Rob:	'sh'
Carl:	((*Writes 's'*)) **Carl is the scribe this time.**
Rob:	'sh' **Prompts to correct Carl. Peer scaffolding.**
Carl:	((*Writes 'sh'*)) (5) 'd' **Gets 3 letters correct but missed one out.**
Rob:	In the middle. **Rob prompts Carl again.**
Carl:	The 'e' comes in the middle and then 'd' at the end. **Carl now gets it right, having had a prompt.**

Rob:	It looks like a Chinese word.
Carl:	It's not a Chinese word.
Rob:	You call it Chinese ((*Laughing*)).
Teacher:	Next word we're going to have a go at is pass (5) <u>pass.</u>
Carl:	I'm sweating. (10) P P P P-A P-A-S ((*Sounds out*))
Rob:	((*Writes 'p'*))
Carl:	It's 'a'
Rob:	It's not a 'a'.
Carl:	It is.
Rob:	'e' 'e' 'e'
Carl:	It's not a 'e' it's a 'a'
Rob:	((*Writes 'a'*))
Carl:	's' 's' 's' that's a 's'
Rob:	((*Writes 's'*))
Carl:	That's not a 's'
Rob:	((*Holds up 'pas' on his whiteboard, looks at teacher's 'pass'*))
Carl:	((*Rubs it out*)) I'm collecting the boards.

Task Two (Track 17) 2 minutes
Mandy   Zoe

Whole class on the carpet, teacher explicitly told children to discuss a recount, in pairs.
((*Whispering to each other, too quiet to hear first few sentences*))

Mandy:	They went to the fire station.
Zoe:	A big place.
Mandy:	They sat by the wheel.
Zoe:	Remember a man read a story and he jumped off and drawed a picture.
Mandy:	He went up a pole.
Zoe:	And grabbed it dead quick.
Mandy:	And then let go and slide down.
Zoe:	He let go fast and fell down.
Mandy:	He got a bit scared.
Zoe:	They got a ladder.
Mandy:	Then he went to get ice cream.
Zoe:	And went on a bouncy castle.

Task Three (Track 18) 2 minutes
Molly   Jade

Teacher explicitly told children work together to sequence events.

Molly:	erm what it's about is they went to get ice cream.
Jade:	((*Laughing*)) The bouncy castle and got some ice cream. **Jade builds on Molly's contribution.**
Molly:	He might have gone the shops then. Ha! There's the mike. ((*Pointing at the microphone*)) **Distracted by research process.**
Jade:	erm (5) He went to the Isle of Man.
Molly:	Bouncy castle, ice cream and the shop. **Lists elements.**
Jade:	Er a man went on the pulley.
Molly:	A little boy went on the pulley. **Corrects Jade.** If you want it to go up you have to pull it that way, if you want to go down you let go of it a bit of the time.
Jade:	If you want it to go up that way you pull it down. **Continues what Molly was saying.**
Molly:	It was an open day. **Molly now gives a new recollection.**
Jade:	Everyone went to the fire station. The man said do you want to go in the tractor and he said yea and the man helped him get in.
Molly:	In the thingio where you drive it. **A sequence of events.**
Jade:	Molly's talking in that. ((*Pointing to the microphone and laughing*)) **Distracted by research process.**

Task Four (Track 19) 20 minutes

Judy	Amber	Paula	Tony	Kyle	Adrian

Teacher explicitly told children work together to explain, by taking turns to write sentences, what is happening in some photographs related to the fire station open day. Although the children are taking turns to write in pairs, the group below often refer to each other's work, so the whole group has been transcribed.

Paula:	What's that there?
Judy:	Look it's a microphone.
Adrian:	It's in the middle.
	((*Paula singing in background ah ah ah ah ah ah ah*))
	Distracted by research process.
Amber:	They're just photographs.
Paula:	[What shall we write? **Tries to get on with task, asks for help.**
Tony:	Pass me that pencil.]
Judy:	The boy went to the Isle of Man ((*Replies to Paula*)).
	((*Paula chanting in background yeah yeah yeah yeah yeah yeah*))
Amber:	Yeah.
Judy:	((*Writing one word at a time as she said them aloud*)) The-boy-went-to-the-Isle-of-Man. **On task.**
Amber:	[In the summer I went on holiday.
Adrian:	It's a girl.] ((*Referring to Judy's comment*))
Paula:	No.
Adrian:	The one in the green jacket is the boy. **Corrects Judy.**
Judy:	The girl went to the (5) oh yeah. **Judy agrees with Adrian.**
Tony:	I'm writing loads. **Is he copying out what Judy said?**
Kyle:	((*Writing but not speaking*)) **ditto**
Paula:	On **Makes a suggestion.**
Adrian:	Holiday. ((*Spells it out*)) H-O-L- **Carries on the sentence.**
Paula:	'i' hol – i – day (5) in the summer. **Helps with spelling.**
Kyle:	I went to the fire station. **Makes a suggestion.**
Judy:	It's your turn.
Amber:	There is a fire engine. **Makes an alternative suggestion.**
Judy:	No no no no no. **Disagrees**.
Paula:	What's it called again? **Tries to clarify.**
Adrian:	He went to the fire station in the Isle of Man. **Puts a whole sentence together combining their ideas.** (5) You've done yours small we've done ours big.
Amber:	The boy (10) let me think of it meself (.) don't think of it all for me.
Adrian:	It's not a race. **Suggests collaboration rather than competition.**
Kyle:	I know.
Adrian	…went…
Amber:	What did you say for the last one?
Judy:	The boy went to (5) the boy went to the fire station in the Isle of Man (.) T-H-E ((*Spells it*)). **Reiterates.**
Paula:	I know how to spell that.
Amber:	((*Writing pul*))
Paula:	((*Reads out P-U-L*))
Amber:	Pulley.
Paula:	He went on the pulley. **Suggests next sentence.**
Adrian:	You forgot don't you?
Paula:	erm
Adrian:	Okay okay. Erm what do I write::: next? (5) He holded the hose pipe. **Suggests next sentence.**
Amber:	<He> went to the (.) he went <TO>
Paula:	Stop telling us what to do.
Adrian:	He sprayed the hose pipe. **Improves on his previous suggestion.**
Amber:	How do you spell station?
Judy:	((*Spells word*)) S-T-A-I-O-N
Amber:	Does that spell station?
Judy:	Put a 't' ((*Watches Amber*)) **Peer support.**

Amber:	Rubber rubber rubber.
Judy:	Don't do a capital letter.
Amber:	[I've done that right.
Kyle:	I don't know what to write.]
Adrian:	((*Writes w-a-r-t-e-r*)) W-A-R-T-E-R.
Paula:	((*Bangs the rubber*))
Adrian:	<u>Stop it.</u>
Paula:	Put it there ((*Pointing at the 'r' in water*)) **Peer support.**
Adrian:	((*Writes owt of*))
Judy:	You haven't done it right. Do that bit again. **Peer support.**
Amber:	<u>Oh.</u> **Some tension.**
Judy:	Stop arguing. **Some tension.**
Adrian:	You
Paula:	You got the elephants we got the hippos. ((*Pictures on the rubbers*)) **Stray off task briefly.**
Adrian:	<Ah> you done three full stops.
Tony:	I know. ((*Rubbing some out*))
Kyle:	You don't need to rub it out.
Tony:	You can't just cross it out.
Paula:	That's too small.
Amber:	He went on the pulley.
Kyle:	You haven't wrote anything.
Adrian:	Leave a space. ((*Makes a fire engine siren noise x 3*))
Kyle:	((*Talking to Amber*)) Write went on the pulley. **Trying to help.**
Adrian:	<u>the</u>
Paula:	What about went on the (.) engine?
Adrian:	Do <u>fire</u> first. He went in the <fire> engine. **Trying to help.**
Paula:	You forgot the 'r'
Adrian:	I don't know how to spell it.
Kyle:	'u'
Tony:	'u'
Amber:	((*Blows a raspberry*))
Kyle:	((*Spells out*)) P-U-L-L-
Judy:	Is that the way you spell engine?
Paula:	I've got engine.
Judy:	I already knew engine.
Kyle:	I'm not copying.
Adrian:	I'm rubbing out the table. ((*Using rubber on table*))
Judy:	Bounce bounce ((*Dropping the rubber*)) He went on the pulley.
Amber:	That's a 'l' 'l'
Paula:	I can write 'on the bouncy castle' up here and leave a space.
Judy:	Look at what I've done. Yous 'av got the same as us.
Kyle:	Fire f-i-r-e station 'st' ((*Putting a finger space to help Tony, who does not write Kyle's word*)) I said 'st' (5) yous are doing it the wrong way. **Trying to help.**
Amber:	We've done more than yours already. **Some tension.**
Paula:	SO. **Some tension.**
Kyle:	((*Helping Tony write*)) That's the end of our sentence. ((*Tony and Kyle get up to show the teacher*))
Amber:	It's my go.
Judy:	[The boy went
Paula:	That's my rubber.]
Kyle:	Elephants.
Adrian:	Have you got engine ((*Looks at sheet to see words*)) YAHOO all done.
Tony:	Give me 5. ((*High hand clap with Kyle and also with Adrian*))
Judy:	We're doing PE outside today. **Stray off task.**
Amber:	I've forgotten me trainers but miss said my shoes will be alright.
Judy:	'Cos year 6 are having their SATs party in the hall. ((*Loud coughing*)) **Still off task.**
Amber:	We'll be using the skipping ropes without the buttons.
Paula:	I'm gonna skip with my drumstick at dinner time. **Still off task.**
Judy:	((*Laughing*)) I'm talking in the mike. **Still off task.**
Teacher:	Asks children to back to the carpet.

| Paula: | I'll bring the work to the carpet and you read your sentence. |
| | ((*Children get up and go to the carpet for the plenary where each group feed back on their work*)) |

They drifted off task at the end but did do what was required of them.

Year 2 Wednesday June 9th – Lesson based on asking questions. (To link with science topic on babies and toddlers, two mums due to come in with baby/toddler, the class were preparing questions to ask them, as research for a book they were planning to write).

Task One (Track 12) 1 minute
Barry   Stuart

Teacher explicitly told children to work in pairs to discuss suitable questions for a selection of headings (communicating, playing, keeping clean, eating, sleeping, moving) to ask the mums, who were due to come into school.

Barry:	How do babies communicate?
Stuart:	They're copying ours. **More concerned about another pair.**
Barry:	What do babies eat? **Comes up with a second question.**
Stuart:	So, you're doing that one (5) you're only meant to do one. **Still more concerned with other things and has made no contribution.**
Barry:	Blah blah blah blah.
Stuart:	erm.
Barry:	You do one. **Tries to make Stuart take a turn.**
Stuart:	Why do babies sleep?

Task Two (Track 13) 5 minutes
Norman   George

Teacher explicitly told children to work with their writing partner (sharing a white board and taking turns to write) to make a question they could ask the mums, who were due to come into school.

Norman:	He's not letting me work with him. ((*Turning to teacher*)) **A tense start.**
George:	I am. ((*Gives Norman the Whiteboard*))
Norman:	When do babies usually communicate? ((*Starts writing it down*)) **Thinks of question and starts to write it down.**
George:	((*Spells out word*)) B-A-B-Y NO I-E-S C-O-M-M-U-N-I-C-A-T-E **Helps Norman by sounding out spellings.**
Norman:	You need to write a question. **Wants George to think of a question.**
George:	((*starts to write*)) How do babies eat? ((*Norman watches George write*)) ((*Another child accuses this pair of copying*))
Norman:	We've done our own question, not yours ((*Turning to another pair*))
George:	Shall we do another one? **On task.**
Norman:	Yes. Do babies communicate at night?
George:	You writ that too big. **Arguing again.**
Norman:	It's not. **More tension.**
George:	How do babies communicate? **Back on task.**
Norman:	Leave a finger space. ((*Pointing to whiteboard*)) **Suggestion.**
George:	What are you trying to do? I am. **Not keen on suggestion.**
Norman:	Nah. I'll show you. **Insists on intervening.**
George:	What's next? **Is again keen to do more.**
Norman:	How do babies eat? ((*Writes sentence*))
George:	I don't feed them.
Norman:	How many shall we do? **On task.**
George:	BABIES BABIES BABIES
Norman:	We can spell babies. I-E-S I-E-S
George:	How do babies sleep **Thinks of another question.**
Norman:	Question mark. **Helps with punctuation.**

Task Three (Track 14) less than 1 minute
Ben   Roger

Teacher explicitly told children to work together to choose one question the pair would like to ask the mums.

Ben: My question.
Roger: No mine.
Ben: Mine's better.
Roger: No I'm having my question.

Teacher stopped class because too many children were arguing. End of shared session.

Task Four (Track 15) 15 minutes
Bill   Tom   Brenda   Mabel

Independent/group work. Teacher asked the children to work in groups with flip chart paper and markers. Each table had its own heading (communicating, playing, keeping clean, eating, sleeping, moving) and they had to devise questions for the mums of a baby and a toddler on their heading.

Tom: When does Brenda go?
Bill: My turn after you.
Brenda: Why don't you do one? (15) When do babies bath? ((*Tom writes the question*))
Mabel: How do babies keep clean? ((*Starts to write*))
Tom: Write yours there. ((*Pointing to the sheet*))
Bill: Hurry up. It's my turn after you. **Tension.**
Tom: No it goes round in a circle. Tension.
Bill: Okay. It's me after. **Tension.**
Brenda: My turn after you. **Tension.**
Bill: You're handwriting's small. **Tension.**
Brenda: I like Tom's handwriting.
Tom: AH. Look what you've done. ((*Bill had grabbed pen and written on Tom's jumper*)) **Tension.**
Mabel: When do babies have their ((*Tom interrupts*)) **Tries a question**.
Tom: How do babies keep their teeth clean?
Brenda: Put a question mark. **Prompts.**
Mabel: It's like this. ((*Points at one*)) **Helps**.
Bill: My turn. (10) How does a baby wash its hair? ((*Writing*))
Tom: How do you spell does? ((*Writes dose*)) **Asks for help.**
Mabel: Give the pen to Brenda. **Trying to give children their turn.**
Brenda: My question (.) what shall I do?
Tom: What about their tummy?
Mabel: What about the bath?
Brenda: Who keeps (5) Who keeps babies clean? ((*Writes while others watch*))
Bill: Which babies keep clean? ((*Laughing*)) Where do babies keep clean?
Tom: I'll do mine next. (5) Mine's (.) when-do-babies-keep-clean?
Brenda: ((*Spells out*)) B-A-B-I-E-S   C-L-E-A-M ah N
Tom: ((*Changes M to N and passes Bill the pen*)) Do your writing <u>now</u>. What do babies keep clean?
Bill: ((*Writes*)) How do babies keep clean on their own?
Brenda: How do babies keep their hair clean? ((*Writes*))
Mabel: ((*Sounds out*)) H-I-A-R   H-A-I-R
Brenda: The hair on your head.
Tom: Don't do yours too big.
Mabel: I'll hold the paper.
Bill: Come on.
Mabel: Can I take a different turn? ((*Tom grabs pen*))
Tom: <u>Why</u> do babies keep clean? ((*Writing*))
Brenda: I've got penguins in me house. **Off task.**
Tom: You haven't. **Off task.**
Mabel: She 'as. **Off task.**

Bill:	Nah. **Off task.**
Mabel:	I've seen 'em, they're chocolate biscuits. **Off task.**
Tom:	Whose go is it now? **Tries to get group back on task.**
Brenda:	I can smell pen. **Still off task.**
Tom:	((*Colours in spaces in writing*)) **Off task.**
Mabel:	How do babies keep their hands clean?
Bill:	We haven't done enough.
Mabel:	How do
Tom:	((*Knocking the table*)) **Tom still off task.**
Mabel:	<u>Stop it Tom.</u> How do babies keep their feet clean?
Tom:	That's not spelt right. **Having been told off by Mabel, now intervenes.**
Bill:	MY GO ((*Tom snatches pen*)) **Tension.**
Brenda:	We've done enough. **Still off task.**
Tom:	Shall I take another turn? **Wants another go.**
Brenda:	Mr Midgy. **Tension again.**
Bill:	Na na na na na na na na ((*Sings Batman tune*)) **Off task.**
Tom:	It's an emergency.
Brenda:	Be quick I want another go.

Teacher calls them for the plenary.

Year 3 Friday June 11th – Lesson based on a poem - *Custard the Dragon.*

Task One (Track 22) 2 minutes
Olivia   Jess

Teacher explicitly told children to work with the person next to them, to clap and count syllables on line one of the poem.

Jess:	Syllables.
Olivia:	((*Sings and claps first line*)) Be-lin-da lives in a little white house
Jess:	No **Disagrees.**
Olivia:	9 syllables (.) put 9
Jess:	There's 2 in little (5) ((*Claps*)) lit-tle there's 2 in little **Corrects Olivia.**
Olivia:	((*Recites again*)) Be-lin-da lives in a lit-tle white house **Gets it right.**
Jess:	There's 10 **Correct answer through peeer support.**
Olivia:	We're on the second sentence now.
Jess:	I've just wrote it down (.) it's 10 look look
Olivia:	I'm doing the second sentence.
Jess:	I've done it. (5) There's 13 in the second one.
	((*Teacher went through the first line*))

Background information: the lesson was based on a poem - *Custard the Dragon.* The teacher explicitly told the children to work with the person next to them, to clap and count syllables on line one of the poem.

Task Two (Track 23) 2 minutes
Peter   Alan

Teacher explicitly told children to work in pairs to clap and count syllables on line two of the poem.

Peter:	We do the second line now.
Alan:	with is 1 syllable.
Peter:	((*Reads words*)) with a little black kitten and a little grey mouse.
Alan:	((*Claps along with Peter's reciting*)) **Collaborating.**
Peter:	with 1 a 1 little 1 black 1 kit-ten 2 and 1 a 1 little 1 grey 1 mouse 1
Alan:	lit-tle is 2 ((*Claps twice for little*)) **Helps and corrects.** What's the answer to that?
Peter:	1 2 3 4 5 6 7 8 9 10 11 12 13 (5) There's 13.

Alan:	((*Checks himself*)) with 1 a 1 lit-tle 2 black 1 kit-ten 2 and 1 a 1 lit-tle 2 grey 1 mouse 1
Peter:	Do we do the third line now?
Alan:	Don't do that line yet.
	((*Teacher went through the second line*))

Task Three (Track 24) 3 minutes
Anna   Jemma

Teacher explicitly told children to work in pairs to clap and count syllables on lines three and four of the poem.

Jemma:	((Clapping)) and a 1 2 lit-tle 2
Anna:	((Clapping)) yel-low 2 dog 1 and 1 a 1 lit-tle 2
Jemma:(	(Clapping) red 1 wag-on 2
Anna:	((Clapping)) and 1 a 1 rea-li-o 3 tru-li-o 3
Jemma:	we don't do that line until miss tells you to.
Anna:	we do (5) ((*Writes the numbers 9 10 11 12*))
Jemma:	((Clapping)) lit-tle pet dra-gon 1,2,3,4,5,6,7,8,9,10,11,12,13,14,15,16
Anna:	We've nearly finished.
Jemma:	Drag-on drag-on rea-li-o tru-li-o
Anna:	So 1,2,3,4,5,6,7,8,9,10,11,12
Jemma:	No.
Anna:	12, 12
Jemma:	We're done then.
	((*Another teacher comes into the class*))
Anna:	HOORAY Here's Mr Atkinson.
Jemma:	I want to go to the tennis (5) tennis.
Anna:	Mr Atkinson.
Jemma:	Mr Atkinson (3) he takes us for P.E.
Anna:	We're going to the tennis this afternoon.
Jemma:	What's time?
	((*Teacher went through the third and fourth lines, then moved on to looking at rhyming couplets*))

Task Four (Track 25) 20 minutes
Stephen   Derek   Lisa   Rhiannon

Teacher explicitly told children to work together in a group to select the correct rhyming words to fit into a selection of poems.

Stephen:	Where's the pencil? **Things that delay children from working.**
Lisa:	There's none in there. ((*Stephen goes off to find a pencil*))
Derek:	Write the date and *The Cat in the Tree* ((*Poem title*))
Stephen:	((*Comes back with a pencil*)) Do we work on them?
Derek:	Yeah (10) I can't hear the rhyme.
	((*All silent for 30 seconds while they write the date*))
Lisa:	There's yours. ((*Passes ruler, to underline date*))
	((*Stephen and Rhiannon read silently*))
Stephen:	((*To Derek and Lisa*)) Yous two read that then we'll read it and then we'll talk about it together. **Leads proceedings and confirms it is a collaborative task.**
	((*All reading silently for five minutes*))
Derek:	Stephen, do you want to work with her?
Stephen:	No she won't work with me.
Lisa:	Do you wanna work with him?
Rhiannon:	All together. **Again, confirms it is a collaborative task.**
Stephen:	This morning the cat got stuck in the tree. Dad said right just leave it.
Derek:	The tree was w w wo wobbly, the tree was tall, Mum said for goodness sake don't fall. It's a rhyme be careful not to FALL.
Rhiannon:	Do you underline it there? Do you underline it? **Asks for clarification.**

Lisa:	The what? The rhyming words?
Rhiannon:	Yeah
Lisa:	Miss said put a circle around it. **Recounts their instruction.**
Stephen:	<u>Underline</u>. I'll ask miss. ((*Goes off for a minute, the others wait quietly*)) **Wastes more work time, by attention to probably unnecessary detail.** You do the book first. ((*Not the worksheet that they had been doing, which was the extension activity*))
Rhiannon:	Write no more.
Derek:	Where's that piece of paper?
Lisa:	What are yous writing? You don't write the whole story though you know.
Derek:	I know (2) I'm only writing the Gingerbread Boy.
Stephen:	NOT THAT
Derek:	Give me a rubber. ((*Rubs out*)) ((*Children quiet for a minute*))
Stephen:	Have we said any words? (5) We'll have to talk then. Right. Everyone write this question down and we'll <u>all</u> work together. **Takes the leads again.**
Derek:	No that's stupid. **Disagrees.**
Rhiannon:	It's not, that's us just working on our table isn't it? **Agrees with Stephen.**
Lisa:	Everything we say gets recorded? So that's us being good? **Conscious of the research process.**
Stephen:	When you've writ the question go, I'm done. **Takes the leads again.**
Derek:	Lisa have you writ the question?
Lisa:	I've wrote the gingerbread.
Stephen:	When you've written the question go, I've done it. **Reiterates his instruction.**
Rhiannon:	Is it the first one?
Lisa:	No, we're all working together.
Derek:	I've done the gingerbread man instead of boy.
Stephen:	When you've all done it.
Rhiannon:	Has anyone got a sharpener? **Again, not having equipment to hand, wastes work time.**
Derek:	The Gingerbread Boy was very
Stephen:	Very what Derek?
Lisa:	The Gingerbread Boy was very <u>sad</u>. It's not very bad it's very sad.
Stephen:	Does anyone think the gingerbread boy was a sneak?
Rhiannon:	No, I think he's very clever.
Stephen:	Does anyone think he ran away, and his mum was (5) erm, no no (.) he was very t?
Derek:	No
Stephen:	The gingerbread boy was very clever.
Rhiannon:	Yeah because he's very clever.
Lisa:	No, he's very bad, he's very bad because he's running away.
Rhiannon:	No. He's very clever. Do you know why? Because he's running away and the fox is running away from the woman and he knows the woman is not going to get him, if he's running, isn't it? **Gives a reason for her choice, to try and justify it to the group.**
Derek:	He's bad. He ran way, he's bad.
Rhiannon:	Alright he's bad. **Gives in to another opinion.**
Derek:	Everyone write bad. **Follows a big discussion about the answer.**
Rhiannon:	I already have.
Lisa:	Are we doing very bad?
Derek:	Is everyone on the second one now?
Lisa:	No I'm not. Have we chose bad or clever?
Derek:	Bad.
Stephen:	Come on. Has everyone done yet?
Rhiannon:	I'm on to my second one.
Derek:	That's it then.
Stephen:	He ran away and his mum was – was sad.
Derek:	Don't write it yet because we're all working together. <u>Don't</u> Stephen. **Tension.**
Lisa:	What are you doing Stephen? (5) **Tension.**
Rhiannon:	It could have been very <u>forever</u>. Or very snappy?

Derek:	SNAPPY
	((*30 seconds silence while all are writing, Rhiannon leaves the table*))
Lisa:	We'll have to wait for Rhiannon. ((*She returns*)) What did we chose for number 2?
Derek:	<u>Sad</u> isn't it?
Rhiannon:	Yeah it's sad.
Stephen:	Can we write the next one?
Derek:	No, we're waiting until everyone writes it Stephen.
Stephen:	<u>Come on.</u> **Trying to stay on task and move along.**
	((*Silence for a minute, all are writing*))
Stephen:	Has everyone writ it?
Derek:	What's the third line?
Lisa:	How come you keep writing it Stephen?
Stephen:	YOU'RE WRITING IT aren't ya? **Tension.** (5) He-told-all-the-animals-you-can't-chase-me ((*Says one word at a time while writing them down*)) ((*Muttering for a minute while all are writing*))
Rhiannon:	I think that's <u>You can't catch me.</u>
Stephen:	Is everyone on the next one now?
Lisa:	On the third one yeah. (10) I know what that one is. You can't have me for your tea.
Rhiannon:	You chose tea?
Lisa:	((*To Stephen*)) Have you wrote tea?
Derek:	What's – that? Is that an 'l' or an 'a'?
Lisa:	Ah, I know what that one is. You can't have me for your tea.
Stephen:	Don't write it yet. (Pause 10) Don't write it yet. **Dominates.**
Derek:	I know, I'm going slowly. **Complies.**
Stephen:	Have you changed the tea in that one?
Derek:	Tea – tea
Stephen:	Don't write it yet. **Dominates again.**
Derek:	Why? **Tension.**
Lisa:	<u>Wait</u> wait. **Tension.**
Derek:	I've writ it. **Tension.**
Lisa:	You need to wait. **Tension.**
Stephen:	He's writ it. **Tension.**
Rhiannon:	He hasn't. **Tension.**
	((*Work in silence for 1 minute*))
Lisa:	Red fox (15) I know what that one is, write clever, isn't it?
Rhiannon:	Why have you chose clever anyway?
Derek:	We would have been past it.
Stephen:	With a (5) with a snip and a snap, ((*sounds* out)) s-n-i-p
Lisa:	You have to do the explanation mark you know. **Corrects.**
Teacher:	Okay, put your pencils down.
Stephen:	Miss, can't we do just this one?
Teacher:	[<5-4-3-2-1>
Derek:	He was -]
Lisa:	was gone
Derek:	'g'
Lisa:	forever
Derek:	What is it?
Stephen:	Forever
Derek:	Done it.
Stephen:	We've finished.
Teacher:	Pencils down.

There are things that prevent children from working, usually minor things, but that are nevertheless disruptive.

Rhiannon:	Do you underline it there? Do you underline it? **Asks for clarification.**
Lisa:	The what? The rhyming words?
Rhiannon:	Yeah.
Lisa:	Miss said put a circle around it. **Recounts their instruction.**
Stephen:	<u>Underline.</u> I'll ask miss. ((*Goes off for a minute, the others wait quietly*)) **Wastes more work time, by attention to probably unnecessary**

detail. You do the book first. ((*Not the worksheet that they had been doing, which was the extension activity*))

This group task also shows moments of tension.

Derek:	I've writ it. **Tension.**
Lisa:	You need to wait. **Tension.**
Stephen:	He's writ it. **Tension.**
Rhiannon:	He hasn't. **Tension.**

Although this could be disputational talk, which is unproductive, the group do get their work done. This is mainly through cumulative talk where they confirm each other's views without challenge but there is also a sequence of exploratory talk, where group members offer different answers and try to justify their choice to the others.

Rhiannon:	Yeah because he's very clever.
Lisa:	No, he's very bad, he's very bad because he's running away.
Rhiannon:	No. He's very clever. Do you know why? Because he's running away and the fox is running away from the woman and he knows the woman is not going to get him, if he's running, isn't it? **Gives a reason for her choice, to try and justify it to the group.**
Derek:	He's bad. He ran way, he's bad.
Rhiannon:	Alright he's bad. **Gives** in to another opinion.
Derek:	Everyone write bad. **Follows a big discussion about the answer.**

Lisa offered the answer 'sad', Rhiannon and Stephen thought 'clever', then Lisa explained why the Gingerbread boy was 'bad' and Rhiannon justifies why she thinks the answer is 'clever'. Derek finally says 'bad' is the answer and the others give in to this view. For once, Derek has had the final say, rather than Stephen, who usually is dominant in the group. Generally, working as a group supported rather than hindered task completion, as children did support each other, but pairs might have been a way of getting more work done with less tension.

Year 4 Tuesday June 8th – Lesson based on a persuasive writing poster.

Task One (Track 7) 1 minute
Carl   Emma

Teacher explicitly told children to work in pairs to predict what the poster was about from looking at the pictures.

Carl:	It's about litter, like a litter bug.
Emma:	It could be about someone writing a letter and not knowing what to write.
Carl:	I've got a desk like that. **Not relevant to task.**
Emma:	Someone erm wrote a letter and threw it in the bin.
Carl:	It's about recycling.
Emma:	It could be about making things, there's card and paper and stuff.

Task Two (Track 8) 1 minute
Sean   Kelly

Teacher explicitly told children to work in pairs to decide what persuasion is.

Sean:	When you want someone to do something like save trees.
Kelly:	But you need trees to help you live like oxygen.
Sean:	But nature's done that.
Kelly:	It's like, you want someone to do something like save trees so you try to persuade them to do what you want.
Sean:	It's like when you try to make someone do something.

112

Task Three (Track 9) 1 minute

Amy   Ian

Teacher explicitly told children to work in pairs on facts and opinions.

Amy: A fact is like on the news.
Ian: Facts are something that does happen.
Amy: So many stuff in books.
Ian: Like in science.
Amy: I'm happy is my opinion.
Ian: It's a way of looking at it.
Amy: Opinions doesn't happen.
Ian: A fact is like the truth and that, an opinion is like when I say I like a top in a shop and then Amy comes over and says she does not like it.
Amy: A fact is a true sentence.
Ian: A fact is a piece of information.

Task Four (Track 10) 15 minutes

Wendy   Alan   Colin   Harry

Teacher asked the children to identify, with different coloured crayons, the opening statement, argument and closing statement in a photocopied piece of persuasive text and pick out 2 key points in argument. Initially did not mention working collaboratively but after 2 minutes told them they could work with each other.

Wendy: ((*Rattling crayons*)) What colours do we use?
Alan: Doesn't matter.
Colin: What's the title?
Wendy: Pass me the blue.
Harry: Sugar's bad for your teeth.
Alan: Do you have to write in the middle?
Colin: You have to write.
Alan: Just get different colours.
Wendy: I need a sharpener.
Colin: Just keep taking different colours.
Wendy: What's the date?
Alan: Have you got a rubber?
Colin: What?
Harry: Circle the arguments.
Wendy: Which bit?
Alan: It's normally the first part that, sugar is bad for you.
Harry: No it's not the first part.
Alan: I don't want to do that bit yellow.
Colin: Facts here.
Wendy: What's that again?
Alan: You have to underline, like.
Harry: That labels that section.
Wendy: Rubber.
Alan: I want the sharpener.
Colin: Who's got the rubber?
Harry: Look that's the argument.
Colin: What's that?
Wendy: It's too hard.
Colin: What?
Alan: That's the hardest colour.
Colin: That's alright now.
Alan: Pass that blue. ((*Tapping pencils*))
Wendy: What does conclusion mean?
Harry: I know.
Wendy: Harry, tell us what conclusion means.
Alan: A bit of help please if you know what conclusion means.
Harry: It's when some has had an argument.
Wendy: It's like stopping an argument.

Alan:	Or it's the person that told you something.
Colin:	How do you spell it?
Wendy:	I'll have to read some of this.
Harry:	That's information.
Wendy:	((*Constant noise from banging and dropping crayons and pencils*))
Alan:	Put a question mark.
Colin:	I think I know what the whole argument is.
Harry:	I know what the argument is, it's don't eat lots of sugar because it's bad for your health.
Colin:	Sugar is bad for your teeth and it will cause tooth decay. A sticky substance on your teeth called plaque I reckon.
Alan:	The argument is the end bit.
Colin:	No.
Harry:	The end bit is the conclusion.
Colin:	The middle bit is the argument.

Year 5 Tuesday June 8th – Lesson based on *Charlotte's Web*.

Task One (Track 4) 5 minutes

James   Sophie   Megan   Beth

The teacher explicitly told the children to discuss vocabulary in groups and decide whether it was 1950s, American or simply unfamiliar to them.

James:	Papa.
Sophie:	That's the Spanish word for Dad.
Megan:	And sneakers.
Beth:	Pop or Pops.
Megan:	I've never heard of Papa.
Beth:	There's this little girl in our Morris Dancing, right =
James:	Blissful.
Beth:	= and she calls him Pops.
James:	Specimen.
Megan:	I've never heard of that.
Sophie:	I have.
Megan:	Rump.
James:	Pitcher, a pitcher of cream, a pitcher. P-I-T-C-H-E-R. Like in American golf or cricket.
Megan:	Sneakers.
James:	Hoghouse. They call it hogs, we call it erm pigs.
Megan:	What does runt mean again?
Sophie:	Little runt.
Megan:	Beth just tapped me. ((Laughing))
James:	You're going to get caught on tape.
Beth:	What's arable?
James:	Do away with it.
Megan:	ARABLE.
Beth:	Vocabularyaryary.
Sophie:	Stop it Beth.
Beth:	I can't say it.
Sophie:	Anyway, you need to find vocabulary words, okay?
Megan:	That we don't know.
James:	Injustice.
Sophie:	We call it something else over here.
Megan:	I've got one…
Beth:	I'm saying knickers.
James:	That's an English word, I've heard that one before.

They were co-operative, but did not have enough background knowledge to work out whether the vocabulary was 1950s or American.

Task Two (Track 5) 15 minutes

David   Jenny   Sarah   Rachel   Julie

Teacher explicitly told children to discuss 2 different viewpoints/persuasive arguments (for and against killing the pig), refer to text and write notes on white boards. Told to work in pairs but worked as a group.

David:	((*So much background noise, unable to hear the first few minutes*))
Jenny:	((*So much background noise, unable to hear the first few minutes*))
Sarah:	((*So much background noise, unable to hear the first few minutes*))
Rachel:	((*So much background noise, unable to hear the first few minutes*))
Julie:	((*So much background noise, unable to hear the first few minutes*))

David:	The microphone is on, it's recording. It's the point of view of her Dad.
Jenny:	She doesn't want the pig to die.
David:	But the Dad wants to get rid of it.
Sarah:	Fern says to the Dad…
Rachel:	It's an argument.
David:	Persuasive. Fern doesn't want any of the animals to die.
Jenny:	Are you gonna right that down?
David:	It's a point of view.
Sarah:	That is a point of view.
Rachel:	We have to do our work.
Julie:	That's why we always get split up, cos we're talking at the same time.
Jenny:	She makes a point, doesn't she though?
David:	What type of language is it?
Julie:	Persuasive.
David:	Her Dad thinks that the pig should just be killed.
Sarah:	I've got it on video.
Rachel:	I think she's got a point.
Julie:	She is making a point to her Dad.
Jenny:	Just read a bit more.
Sarah:	Are you listening to this? I think that Fern should not keep the pig.
David:	The Dad's a trouble maker, that's what he thinks.
Jenny:	He's not a trouble maker, the pig is too small.
Sarah:	Like a baby.
Rachel:	I'm not messing.
Julie:	Read it here, too small and could die anyway.
David:	I'm sure it says trouble maker round here.
Jenny:	Whenever she's made a point I wrote it down.
Rachel:	Let Fern look after the pig.
David:	She's linking between her and the pig and she doesn't want the pig to be killed, she makes her points and has a persuasive argument.
Jenny:	If Fern was small, would her father kill her?
Sarah:	It's her birthday and she's invited them.
Julie:	If she was small when born, would her Dad kill her?
Sarah:	It's maths next.
David:	I like maths, maths is gonna get me in to the Bluecoat.
Sarah:	Do you want to go to the Bluecoat?
David:	It's a good school. If you want to be a councillor and get to the top.
Rachel:	Ah, we've spelt Fern wrong.
David:	F-E-R-M no N. (10) The Dad doesn't care does he?
Jenny:	I'm having a pool party this year for my birthday, or a gym party. We want to book this gym thing for tomorrow for an hour.
David:	We're supposed to be working.
Sarah:	I'm writing it down.
Rachel:	la la la la
David:	It would be better if you had a camcorder to make sure you know who is talking.
Jenny:	Whisper about my birthday.
Sarah:	Can you still hear it even if I whisper.
Rachel:	Has it got a sensor?
Sarah:	It's like what they have in the police station.

Rachel:	I listen to what they say on the police scanner.
Julie:	shshshshshshsh!
	((*Teacher stops class, as she says they are going off task*))

Task Three (Track 5) 10 minutes
Eric   Andrew   Hazel

Teacher explicitly told children work together to do a role play showing the character's opposing viewpoints. (Told to work in pairs but neither boy would role play the female character, so teacher asked a girl to join them).

Eric:	Mr Arable is persuasive, persuading his daughter, like, he knows.
Andrew:	He knows, like, how to use them, care for them better than her.
Eric:	Care, like, for his daughter?
Andrew:	Mr Arable persuades…
Eric:	What one is Mr Arable?
Andrew:	I don't want to be Fern.
Eric:	You have to read Fern's out.
Andrew:	No.
Eric:	Control yourself Fern erm it's a matter of life and death.
Andrew:	He tries to persuade his daughter.
Eric:	Start again. Control yourself.
Andrew:	Sobbing and pleading.
Eric:	Control yourself Fern.
Andrew:	Sobbing and pleading.
Eric:	You don't go 'sobbing and pleading'.
Andrew:	I want to be Mr Arable
	((*Teacher asks girl to join the pair to play Fern*))
Eric:	She's Fern.
Andrew:	Did you do any planning for Fern?
Hazel:	I was going to be the pig.
Andrew:	I want to play the pig or Mr Arable.
Eric:	Control yourself Fern.
Hazel:	Don't kill the pig, don't kill the pig.
Eric:	Control yourself.
Hazel:	I can't, I want the pig, you're not killing it.
Eric:	You can't get everything that you want.
Hazel:	I can.
Andrew:	Control yourself Fern.
Hazel:	Control myself, this is a matter of life and death.
Eric:	Say that.
Andrew:	Gizzit.
Hazel:	You's crap.
Eric:	Control yourself.
Hazel:	Control myself, this is a matter of life and death and you tell me to control myself.
Eric:	It's only a pig.
Hazel:	Only a pig. If I was little you wouldn't kill me.
Eric:	((*Laughing*)) I would.
Hazel:	I know you would.
Andrew:	I was thinking of something just then.
Eric:	Control yourself.
Hazel:	Control myself, this is a matter of life and death and you tell me to control myself.
Eric:	I can handle pigs better than you.
Hazel:	I know more about raising a litter of pigs than you do.
Eric:	But I'm a farmer.
Hazel:	So I'm younger. I'm little and you're big and I'm right and you're wrong and there's nothing you can do about it.
Eric:	It's my pig and I'm faster and you're slower.
Andrew:	Will you go out with me?
Hazel:	Ah!

Andrew:	Stinky little runt.
Eric:	You can't persuade me when you are sobbing and pleading.
Hazel:	I see no difference (.) I do it all the time.
Eric:	I will never let you do it again. You can't persuade me I'm your Dad.
Hazel:	You can't persuade me I'm your Daughter.
Eric:	Why can't I?
Hazel:	Because I said so.
Andrew:	That wasn't good ((*Blows a raspberry*)).

Year 6 Thursday June 10th – Lesson based on writing an introduction for a book review of *The Giant's Necklace*.

Task One (Track 20) 15 minutes

| Kaitlin | Sonia | Lydia | Zak | Leon |

Background information – teacher was on supply and had been there for 2 weeks, after a succession of different supply teachers, who could not control the class. He had never tried paired or group work, as the class was hard to manage. Today was the first time the children had been asked to work together. Teacher did not initially tell children they could work in together, but after 5 minutes explained they could work in with the person next to them, talk about the work and read each other's. The children in this group decided to work as a group, rather than in pairs.

Kaitlin:	So erm.
Zak:	Are you putting a voice on? ((*Due to the microphone being there*))
Kaitlin:	Our character is Cherry (5) the settin' is Cornwall.
Zak:	What day is it?
Kaitlin:	Thursday. Thursday the 10th.
Zak:	I thought it was Wednesday.
Lydia:	It was Wednesday yesterday.
	((*30 seconds silent pause, while the children wrote the date*))
Kaitlin:	She's (.) she's collecting (.) what do you call it? Cowry shells.
Leon:	What do we call it? (5) The Giant's Necklace.
Kaitlin:	The shells, pink cowry shells.
Zak:	We've done this three times (10) oh no, we're only doing the introduction. (5) Can we copy that first? ((*Teacher's writing on the board*)) We'll start it like that and then continue it ourselves.
Kaitlin:	Urgh. The pencil touched me lip.
Zak:	Do that. ((*Referring to teacher's first sentence on the board*)) The author takes the story of the Giant's Necklace and then continue it, isn't it? (5) <u>Do that first.</u>
Kaitlin:	How do you spell author?
Zak:	((*Spells it out*)) A-U-T-H-O-R
	((*Teacher now tells children they can work together*))
Kaitlin:	((*Writing as she* speaks)) The author takes the story (5) to be finished. **Keeping to task and thinking aloud, as it is a group task.**
Zak:	So the author takes the story of the Giant's Necklace **Adds something and displays keeping to task.**
Leon:	and they just go to Cornwall. **Adds something else, keeping to task.**
Zak:	Yeah (.) to be finished.
Kaitlin:	yet to be finished. **Improving on Zak's and keeping on task.**
Leon:	No, do that in brackets. **Makes a suggestion.**
Zak:	is yet to be finished. I'm roasting. ((*Takes off jumper*)) Yet to be finished <u>comma</u> and then to Cornwall <u>full stop</u>. **Zak does not do Leon's brackets, he uses commas.**
Leon:	washed out to sea at the end. **Again Leon's comment is ignored.**
Zak:	So the author takes the story of the Giant's Necklace comma which is <u>yet</u> to be finished comma to Cornwall full stop. **Reiterates work agreed so far.**
Kaitlin:	((*Writing as she says the* words)) which is yet to be finished to Cornwall (.) Full stop? **Questions Zak's choice of punctuation.**

Zak:	Yeah 'cos there's too many commas. **Zak gives an explanation.**
Leon:	in Cornwall (.) You should do that in brackets. **Tries again for brackets.**
Kaitlin:	Why what are we doing now?
Zak:	Are you finished? (5) when she's washed out? **Refers back to Leon's earlier comment...**
Leon:	No you can't do that it's at the end. ... **but Leon says it can't go there.**
Zak:	Yeah we could do when a little girl named Cherry is collecting her pink cowry shells for her necklace which is big enough to fit a giant.
Lydia:	So next write
Zak:	NO ((*Says each word slowly with gaps between to write it down*)) <when-a-little-girl-[named]-Cherry-is-collecting-her-> (.) shall we do collecting her precious pink cowry shells?
Leon:	Yeah
Zak:	((*Writing*)) <her-precious-pink-cowry-shells>
Sonia:	((*Just writing, not talking*))
	((*Teacher reminds children that they are supposed to be working together and reading through each other's work*))
Kaitlin:	big enough (.) we're all working together (.) for a giant.
Zak&Kaitlin:	The author takes the story of the Giant's Necklace comma which is yet to be finished comma to Cornwall full stop when a little girl named Cherry is collecting her precious pink cowry shells big enough to fit a giant. **Recap work so far.**
Leon:	Shall I do a comma after shells? **Suggests idea.**
Lydia:	No cowry shells and then brackets. **Makes a different suggestion.**
Zak:	Yeah I reckon we should do that. Leon we're doing this. **Zak listens to Lydia's idea.**
Leon:	Look what we've done. **Clearly proud of the group achievement.**
Lydia:	We're doing commas around from precious or from pink?
Zak:	big enough to fit a giant. ((*Referring to the necklace*))
Lydia:	I've done enough to fit a giant not big enough.
Zak:	I reckon we should do that in brackets (.) which is yet to be finished. The author takes the story of the Giant's Necklace, which is yet to be finished, to Cornwall. When a little girl named Cherry is collecting her precious pink cowry shells, big enough to fit a giant.
Kaitlin:	What can we write now? **Keeping the pace of work moving on.**
Leon:	Cherry did not know there was a storm building up. **Suggestion.**
Kaitlin:	Don't put that yet.
Lydia:	that there was a storm gathering. **Makes an improvement.**
Kaitlin:	She did not know there was a storm coming in. **Gives a different version.**
Zak:	Cherry did not notice that there was a storm gathering up. **Gives another different version, not the best one, but it gets used.**
Leon:	while she was still on the beach. **Makes an improvement.**
Zak:	I'm not doing that I'm just doing there was a storm gathering up. We know she's still on the beach. **Disagrees with Leon's suggestion and gives a reason why.**
Leon:	No we don't. **Leon does not agree with Zak's explanation.**
Lydia:	gathering up on the beach. **Extends the sentence further.**
Leon:	We're probably finished that's enough for the introduction.
Zak:	Later on in the story we find out she's dead.
Leon:	No don't say that 'cos that's a surprise and you'll know that she's dead. **Perceptive comment, relevant to task.**
Zak:	The author is yet to surprise the reader (20) the author (5) the author is yet (5) is yet to surprise the reader on later things to come in the story. **Zak took note of Leon here.**
Leon:	Yeah.
Lydia:	Yeah to <surprise later>.
Zak:	So the author is yet to surprise the reader on later things to come in the story (5) the story full stop that's it. **Has accepted Leon's view that they have done enough and that they should not disclose that the girl is dead.**
Leon:	Are we going on the commentary next?
Zak:	Sir, shall we do the commentary as well?

Teacher:	That's not in the introduction.
Zak:	No we've done the introduction.
Kaitlin:	We've all worked together.

Teacher stopped them for the plenary, where different children read out their review introduction. Teacher commented how working together had brought out more issues, ideas and facts from the story. TA said that it had been the best work done that week.

End of Transcripts

D2   Teacher Interview Questions

Foundation X	KS1	Lower KS2	Upper KS2

Disk 2 ~ Track 3	
1	Do you think speaking and listening receives less emphasis than reading and writing, and if so, why?
	Yes it does. I think really its more historical, children had to sit and listen, and they learn as the teacher taught, and there was no interaction. And I think really that's carried on a little, and in the classroom as well I think sometimes, especially at KS2, I think teachers are sometimes frightened that the taught what's going on isn't necessarily what they want to hear or want it to be about. **Very true.**
2	In your opinion, are there any factors to do with the school or local area that affect children's speaking and listening skills?
	Yes... well, when the children come into Nursery, very few of them have got good language skills, they're very very poor... basically the children aren't spoken to at home... but I don't think the parents converse either. I think it tends to be, if they are at home it's television or videos... and parents don't seem to sit and have conversations, they just shout or scream at one another, fight, bark orders, and just watch the telly or go out. **Yes, so really not having anything modelled for them.** No... not all of them, some of the families are very nice, and there's a huge variation in ability, we've got some who can come in and hold a conversation like an adult, at three, and there are others who just can't string three words together. So I think it is a social thing and a lot of these parents now, and I'm speaking for the children who come into the Foundation Stage, we are getting more and more single parents, very young girls... and we have to really teach them how to speak. And also if they do anything and the children say 'why', if they ask a question, 'why', a lot of the parents will just say 'that's why', because the parents can't elaborate on things, and they can't explain things because they don't know and they don't understand. **Do you think they are aware of that themselves?** No, we do point out to them, when we have our little meeting, we do say if the children ask questions, give them an explanation, and If you don't know say I don't know why that happens. But the children themselves, if you as the children a question they will say, that's why... they've got no idea at all.
3	What do you think of the recent box of materials to support speaking and listening?
	I'm not sure if you have seen it, have you looked at the recent box of materials to support speaking and listening? Yes, but that's for KS1 and 2. There's nothing really applicable to the Foundation Stage, we just use what we've got within the Foundation Stage curriculum, but I do have, I had it here to show you, it's called 'I can talk', and it's very simple, but it does give you some guidelines. And there is going to be INSET on speaking and listening.
4	Do you have any concerns about the planning, teaching and assessment of speaking and listening and also children working together?
	Erm... **Or do you feel comfortable with it?** Well I don't feel there's enough, I don't know enough about teaching it really, and I suppose for me to say that, it's very bad because I have to start it off here, I don't think there's been enough done on speaking and listening. The planning of it... we always plan for it, I don't plan in any great detail, I just make notes because basically I know what I want to get out of the conversation but it could always go off on a tangent especially with little ones, so I think you have to be very flexible... and speaking and listening goes on all day here, so its just an integral part of all the areas in the Foundation Stage, and that's the most important, because until a child can speak fluently they can't read or write. **6.00**
5	Do you specifically tell children when they can work together and does this vary according to the lesson?
	That varies according to the activity here, and really... it's difficult because it depends on what stage of development they're at. You may think that children are working together and they're just working alongside. They're doing their own thing along side one another, and unless they've reached a certain of development, you have to work with them and direct them to work in a group. Today, three little boys who will be going into the Reception class got a game out, and played it properly, and they collaborated and talked to one another this

	afternoon while we were doing that, and they're starting to do that now, and they're starting to play certain games where they'll say, maybe with the cars, 'I'll do such and such a thing', and they're talking to one another and interacting, but a lot of them are nowhere near that stage really, but these are three quite mature little boys. Some of the girls actually are quite mature and play together nicely. In the home corner they will talk, issue roles, 'You be the dad and I'll be the mum and this is the baby', but generally they don't, they just play alongside.
6	In your opinion, does collaborative work support or hinder task completion?
	Well I think it helps, erm… not necessarily in the Foundation Stage but generally I think it helps, because there are always children who are weaker in certain areas, who are very reluctant, and I think erm… if they know they've got the support of their peers, then they might be prepared to actually put an idea forward. I've got a little boy in the Nursery who will not speak to an adult, it's all sign language. But I know he can talk and he's fluent because I hear him with other children… and if he was left on his own all the time I would think he couldn't speak at all. **That's interesting.** You learn an awful lot from actually listening to them talking to their peers, you learn a lot more, I think, than what they will tell you. Sometimes you can pass bye children having a conversation, and you think, oh, they have actually grasped that really really well, but they might not be able to tell you that, and they may not be able to show you that in their work, if you are looking for written work or something, but the conversation that's going on.
7	Do you think that children can support each other's learning, and if so, in what ways?
	Erm…. Well, I think they do, they just support on another and they can help one another along, and if they're stuck with something then they will say 'You can do this this this or this'. **Well you said it in the other question.** Yeah, they are given confidence, and it gives them a forum to speak where they probably wouldn't in a different situation, especially if they're friendship groups as well, I think, it depends on the grouping as well doesn't it? Sometimes girls will only speak with girls and boys will only speak with boys, and it depends on the subject, so… there's a lovely example of that actually, last week, or the week before, we finish earlier than the rest of the school, and a parent had come to see the Year 3 teacher, so I just went into class and sat with them while she came out to speak to the parent, and they were playing games, and they were in pairs, and one of the little girls has special needs, and she couldn't really play the game by herself and the other one, she was lovely, she really looked after her and really helped her play the game. Really sweet! And she was absolutely gorgeous with her, so patient. **11.25**
8	Do you feel that children complete their work better when working independently?
	Well that depends as well, some do, some don't like working with other children at all they would rather work on their own. I think really you've just got to have a balance for the different methods so you give everybody the opportunity to work at their best, really. Because you've also got the converse side of it where some children are going to go off at a tangent and talk about was on the telly last night, you know, it is difficult, or it can be quite difficult to keep them on task. So there are certain circumstances where it may be better for them to work independently.
9	What would be the most effective means in developing your skills in planning, teaching and assessing speaking and listening and also promoting collaborative work?
	Erm… I think more training would be helpful, **In what sort? Videos, team working?** I always feel that whatever I'm doing… I'm doing it myself and am I doing it right, and is everyone else doing it this way, and I like seeing videos because I think it confirms what you're doing is right or I'm not doing it right at all! But, I like videos, I like going to visit good practice in other places and chatting with people who have proven good practice, and just… well any training really because I think training should be ongoing and I don't think there's enough of it, I left college 26 years ago so if I'd never had any training since then where would we be? I feel it should be ongoing all the time and there should be a bit more money put into that.
10	How do you plan for speaking and listening activities?
	Speaking and listening goes on in all the areas, so that's are main way really of gaining an insight into the children's learning in the Foundation Stage, by the way they respond, to your questioning or they can give you reasons and things for what they're doing. But there are times… so you put that into your planning generally. My planning for knowledge and understanding of the words… science, we were doing about frogs, well it was all talking really about frogs, looking at frogs, looking at the different stages, what we could see, the development at the different stages, what was different, and it was all talking. But, I do actually plan it into literacy and we do have circle time when children are encouraged to talk and other children are encouraged to listen to what they're saying and to respond accordingly because especially when they're little, you'll be half way through something and somebody

will chirp up, 'My mum is going to such and such a place tomorrow! I bought something from the Kwikie last...', and it's very hard to keep them focused when you're having a conversation, and so what we do we've got a teddy, and most people will probably do it like that, if you've got the teddy you can talk, nobody else can talk until they get the teddy, unless they are responding to that child. And the assessment is the same way we assess everything, we just make a note of it, and if there's a significant change, or a significant development, then we make a note of that and we put in, they have an assessment profile at this stage and we just fill it in then. **So you probably do more assessing of speaking and listening than anybody else would, because of the nature of the Foundation Stage profile?** Yes, we really assess, it's continuous assessment but it's not like... the rest of the school will have to do a lot more written assessment whereas ours isn't like that really.

11	How do you organise and teach speaking and listening activities?
	Not asked because covered earlier.
12	How do you assess speaking and listening activities?
	Not asked because covered earlier.
13	What benefits do you believe can come from collaborative work? a) For the staff. b) For the children.
	For the children, they've got the support, and for the quieter children that's a big help. For the staff, I think sometimes it's easier if you're setting the task and giving little groups of children a task and you're not having to do it over and over and over again, individually, which at our level... sometimes an activity can take a whole week here, and we've only done one activity because you have to work with one child or maybe two children, if you can work with a little group, and get the more the more able children is what we do and get them to buddy up a little bit and say now, if you and you go together, or you help such a body do that because he doesn't know how to do it yet, and that's a big help because you are drawing on their expertise of the children really, plus its good for them, it develops their social skills, their interactive skills. **18.45** Because some children know more than you about certain subjects, like maths (IT). I remember in IT with Year 1, and we had this programme where I knew I could change the background colour, but I couldn't do it, and I spent all my lunch hour trying to change this background colour, whatever it was, and I was still at it when they came in after lunch, and this child walked to me and said, 'Do you know what Miss, if you press that button there it changes the background colour!' So just ask the children!
14	Do you feel under pressure that every child should record something every lesson?
	No... no, but I don't think that at KS1, I can't say for KS2, but definitely at KS1 I don't think they need to record half as much as they do, and I think quality is far better than quantity really. And whilst I quite like the idea of the National Curriculum, giving guidelines on what we are to teach, I don't agree really with the way its done, but we are addressing that in this school as we are going to try and change the way the Literacy Hour, we are going to incorporate other subject's material into it which will be much better really. Why can't you do your literacy in your history? You used to do years ago! And it worked perfectly well! And then somebody comes along and says I've got this idea, you can't do that! **I think there is a balance between the old topic web when you are sometimes struggling to link things and maybe didn't have objectives specifically for geography, you just thought of an overall topic, then it went to everything was separate, and now we've got to go see where we are going in individual subjects but we've got to link them together – it makes more sense for children to have integrated learning.** Well that's what we are working towards now, and really at the Foundation Stage we do that anyway.
15	In what ways do you model speaking and listening? (Compared with how you would in shared reading and shared writing).
	Well we play, we join in with the play, and we try to introduce the correct language, and it can be quite difficult because you don't want to make children feel what they're doing is wrong. But lots of stories, and try to use lots of descriptive language, and I like story anyway, so I think story is very important... songs, rhymes... just general talking time really. We try to talk to them all the time, and if they say something and it isn't correct then you try to repeat that so that it is. (I saw you doing a role play the other day and it went well actually, you were telling which language to use, suggesting it, and then five minutes later they were doing that themselves). It's actually... we had a forest at one stage and we were going on a picnic, and we worked with small groups of children and we actually modelled what we would do going on a picnic, things we needed, we made a list of things we needed, we packed the picnic basket and we went off on the picnic and we talked about the different things, and for a long time after that they played picnics... and we've taken that from their ideas... but they had

	found a blanket and they went off picnicking, so I brought a picnic basket in after that, and they really enjoyed it. So that's another way you know actually it's a way to assess, it's successful because you can see that there actually using your modelling, to go off in their play.
16	How do you foster and promote paired and group work?
	You just encourage them really to play, and what we try to do, we try to allocate tasks, so I might say to a certain four children, 'I would like you to play this game now', or what we normally do, if it's something they haven't done before, I'd say would you like to come and play this game with me? So that you're actually there modelling it, and joining in with the children, and then next time you can say would you like to go and play that game that we played, and then from then on you can say, now such a body has not played that game, why don't you show him how to play it, and it goes on like that. **25.00**
17	What types of speaking and listening activities do you use in different curricular areas? **How do you use speaking and listening across the curriculum?**
	We just do it all the time. Because they can't write, they can draw but not recognisable with their drawings really, some can, as they get older, so the only form of communication is speaking and listening, and a lot of it, they may not be able to speak in sentences but they can they can make themselves generally understood.
18	Do you think the Foundation Stage Curriculum and the NLS give enough objectives and support to plan, teach and assess speaking and listening?
	No not really, there's very little guidance for anything in the Foundation Stage, they tell you what you should achieve and they will give you an example, but they don't really give you a lot of help, you have to find that from other sources.
19	Do you think that the year group children are in makes speaking and listening or collaborative work any more important or difficult to teach?
	I don't think it's any less important, I do think it gets more difficult. I think especially, in year 6, now that must be really difficult to keep them on task... when they're in their final half term and they know they're going to leave and they can't be bothered. In secondary school they deserve a medal! I can't imagine working in a secondary school! You are alright talking to children who are keen and want to be there.
20	Do you have any comments that you would like to add about speaking and listening or children working collaboratively?
	I think here children are generally quite open and will talk, but there are other schools where you walk into a classroom and there's silence, and I think they're frightened to speak to one another because it's wrong, and I think that's quite sad really. **Do you think that's basically down to the ethos of the school or a particular teacher?** Yes, I think a lot of it is quite possibly pressure, and people don't understand the importance of it. Because to be perfectly honest I think now, when students come out of college they are not trained enough, I don't think they've got enough practical training. And they may be really really good at their subject, but I think far too much emphasis is put onto subject, and not enough on the hands-on teaching. Because we've had students here who have been frightened to death saying, 'We don't know how to do that, I don't know how to teach the Literacy Hour'. You need such a lot of practical experience I think to teach in a primary school.

Any supplementary questions used and general comments

Do you think other staff are aware of the Foundation Stage Curriculum?

Yes we make them well aware! We have some nice arguments about it! There are problems, I feel, when you get to Reception, because the reception teacher is under a lot of pressure to conform to the Literacy and Numeracy Strategy, and it isn't always appropriate. I think schools do put Reception teachers under pressure to be more formal, and its very very difficult because you are being pulled form both sides, because the early years people are saying, DON'T, and the school is saying DO, and then you're getting the other people coming in wanting to assess, and saying well 'Nursery and Reception are going to have to be included in this, you're going to have to get formal work off them', and it isn't always appropriate, and it's quite often far more appropriate for the children to talk to you, and you scribe what they say, than for them to attempt to write something down... and the writing can be quite meaningless. I do writing assessments, because I have to do writing assessments, now at the moment as they are doing a garage and it's in role play, they are using the role play to scribble things down, and I will say what have you written there? 'Somebody has come in to buy some new tyres.' That's great, they're writing it down. Sometimes they'll want to write a story, but you might be flogging a dead horse here and you can't get anything out of them, and it's just not appropriate, but because they have to have something written down, to see the level that they're at, and a lot of it is like that in reception with a lot of things. **31'35**

Do you work closely with the reception teacher?
I try to. The poor girl, she's an NQT and she's working very hard. She's just finding it very difficult I think, she says, 'I've got all this work to get through, I've got to do this, this and this'. It's mad that they stop and go into Year 1 and start the National Curriculum, especially in an area like this because the children are at least 12 months behind here, and some of those children going into Year 1 are only just five, and they're not ready for formal… really, some of these children wouldn't be starting school until they go into the juniors! **You mention that as a result they can be branded as thick/Special Needs.** Now I've got children who I say come and write down, and they can't write. In an area like this, emergent writing is all well and good, and I encourage the children to do lots and lots of scribbling, a lot of the children here have got no idea of letters and sounds, they're not at that stage of development yet… some are very very good, there's a handful that are good, some are hopeless. But if I send home something that they've done, it's not respected, the parents don't look at it and say 'Isn't that lovely' it's a 'phph…' These parents need it to be… they would rather have a pre-printed picture coloured in than a drawing that the child's done. And their name has got to be perfect or they'll say 'You haven't done that right', so a lot of it really is educating the parents as well.
Do you have any after school, not clubs, but where parents can come in and you can work with the parents?
We have done some but the response isn't generally very good either. It's always the one you target who don't want to know! Every week the children in the Nursery take home a story book, they choose any book they like out of the library and get 'That was too hard', and I say, you don't have to read the book, just talk about the pictures. I've sent a note home and I explain to them but they don't listen. And story sacks, we've made a couple of story sacks but I'm very reluctant to send them home because we just don't get them back and the books that come back are absolutely ruined. And when you are spending £50 or £60 on a story sack, we use them in school. **Total time 35:40**

Teacher Interview Questions

Foundation	KS1 X	Lower KS2	Upper KS2

Disk 1 ~ Track 29 and Disk 2 ~ Track 1	
1	Do you think speaking/listening receives less emphasis than reading and writing, if so, why?
	Yes, as an infant teacher I think speaking and listening is more important than anything else, at all. More important than learning to read, write, because once they're speaking they're starting to understand, putting what they're saying into context, making sense of it, thinking, and doing the sort of things they do when they're learning to read. They're thinking before they say things, they're making it make sense, they don't sound it out or spell it out when they're saying it but that kind of thing. And it does not receive as much emphasis as it should do, because it is often seen as an infant thing, and as the majority of literacy advisers are junior trained, that's the main problem. **So it has less status?** Very much so.
2	In your opinion, are there any factors to do with the school or local area that affect children's speaking and listening skills?
	Yes, the area we are in here now, the area the children live in, speech development is very poor, because the majority of the children don't really get spoken to, and if they get spoken to it's just to be shouted at, but not all. You can pinpoint the children whose parents take time out. You can always pinpoint the children, always. I think it effects their learning a great deal, because if you've got children coming into nursery going, ug, ug, ug, it takes a lot longer for them to understand what we want of them. I would say that usually, if they come in an area like this and they have poor speech skills, and listening skills, I could say they are a good year behind a child who's in a leafy suburb. And it doesn't get the recognition off Ofsted, and the people who think they can tell us what to do, which annoys me, having taught in both types of schools.
3	What do you think of the recent box of materials to support speaking and listening?
	Well, I actually got it down from the net a few months ago, no, a couple of months ago I think, and I read through it, and then we got the box, so it's something I have read and it's got some brilliant ideas, things I would not have thought of. There's a particular thing in the drama when they read a book and they have to do freeze frame. I have only read Year 1 but I thought that was superb, and I thought, I'm going to start, I'm going to do that, I'm going to have a real good go, it was something that you wouldn't have thought of yourself, not necessarily, but someone, some boffin has really come up trumps with that, I've thought it's been really good and it's very, very helpful, but it's something I've been aware of for the last couple of months, but I decided to incorporate it in September because I've had maternity leave and so I have not had the chance. **So do you think the school will actually get specific training?** Yes, because the literacy adviser is very much into speaking and listening! She really is.
4	Do you have any concerns about the planning, teaching and assessment of speaking and listening and also children working together?
	The planning... when I plan a speaking and listening I just put... I just say, we're talking in partners, when in with my weekly literacy plan, but, I think maybe, you can go into a little more depth but not too much depth because we've got enough to do anyway. **5:00** So maybe if we had a little speaking and listening box in the literacy plans and say just made bullet points of that, and that would cover the speaking and listening I think for the week, because I am out planned. **(recap of question)** Assessment yes because it's not something I have formally done, I've done it very informally, and with my TA, we've discussed it, we've done a lot of teaching and role play and all that kind of thing, but I've not formally assessed to be perfectly honest. **Do you have any written notes or anything at all?** No, no I don't because it's in with my head.
5	Do you specifically tell children when they can work together and does this vary according to the lesson?
	Yes, it depends, for literacy we do an awful lot working in pairs and working in groups, maths we do. For the science, I intend to work in groups, the likes of the history and geography, if they are doing written work it's independent but I do encourage a discussion, and we do some hot seating sometimes as well, not just in the literacy but we do hot seating in history which they really enjoy, and we use the artefacts as well, and they act it out as well, they did it for Ofsted last year, it went down a bomb, they really enjoyed it. I encourage them to work together if at all possible, and they are told, especially if they look at a piece of work and they go Oh! I say, it's okay, you can work together, I don't mind, especially if it's not an assessment or anything like that, and it's just a little piece of work that they have to just get on with and do. **7:25 So, if it were an assessment**

		though, would you feel differently about how you wanted them to work? Yes, that's what we do, we're assessing at the moment and they're not allowed to work together, although they do try sometimes!
6		In your opinion, does collaborative work support or hinder task completion?
		Support… support completely but you do have to at them, just to remind them that they are doing some work and they're not having a chin-wag. But I can understand how people feel it could hinder them because I'm used to a noisy classroom, and we're a very, not loud, but noisy, bubbly, chatty - as I am myself and I think that it reflects how I am and I do like listening to the children talking. **You can understand why people may be more worried about it?** Yes, I can understand, I understand because as you get further up the school there is that emphasis on being quiet, and getting on with your work, and not copying and not working independently. Whereas it's a pity really because a lot of the foundation and core subjects would benefit from collaborative work.
7		Do you think that children can support each other's learning, and if so, in what ways?
		Yes, it can help with speaking and listening, it can help formulate their ideas, especially with things like maths, it's not just literacy it's maths as well. You buddy them up and get children who are not always as clever at maths as others or their writing, but they help each other, its support as well and they give each other ideas. I just get a lot out of it and I know the children do. They enjoy it greatly.
8		Do you feel that children complete their work better when working independently?
		Some children do, you always get at least three or four in a class and they're usually the brighter children, who don't want to share their ideas and just want to get on with it. I've got one girl in my class who's extremely bright, and will work and will work very well together. She will work in groups or in pairs but there are some things she loves getting on with it, at the moment, when we have busy books when we come in the morning when they are allowed to write and draw for 10 minutes of whatever they like, she got a new busy book the other day and she's writing a book! And she just gets on with it, does it herself, and that's it. I think the less able tend to want to work in groups more and work with partners because it gives them encouragement and it gives them feeling things safe, not getting shouted at, and not feeling silly if they get an answer wrong, they can talk to their friends and it can be like 'I didn't realise that', 'I thought I got it right', it gives them a little bit of satisfaction.
9		What would be the most effective means in developing your skills in planning, teaching and assessing speaking and listening and also promoting collaborative work?
		Taking on board the speaking and listening ideas that I've been reading about. Maybe introducing, as I said, the little box in the corner of a weekly plan, just to have bullet points. I think some formal assessment might be in order but we would have to be quite straightforward, it's not something that would take me ages to do, like a tick sheet, you would do every half-term or every term, and maybe different coloured pens for each half-term or term or whatever. But definitely something like a tick sheet, or maybe a little thing for comments or whatever, but at the end or the day I always ask myself about assessment, who is the assessment actually for? I have a problem with that, because as a teacher, when you go up to your class, I don't personally ever hardly look at last year's assessment. Within three or four days you have got the class sussed, I think. You assess them all the time, and it's helpful to have written assessment for the management. **(End of tape) 12:48** Lots of training is good as well, we need lots of training because this is the thing that's coming up to forefront and our Literacy Advisor knows that and she was talking about it the other day. We were talking about, we had an Inset day high jacked by something else, well we had part of the Inset day high jacked by something else but it was still literacy! So she didn't feel like she did everything that she needed to do so she's… if you've got someone who's very into it, it makes a lot of difference and she's a young teacher as well so we will get the training, training will happen I know it will, and I'm a PSHE Coordinator as well, so I'm really into all that kind of thing and I'll be pushing for circle time throughout the school, and all that kind of thing. I want In-service as well and I've got an expert who will come in and do In-service from the LEA, and she said she would come in and do it anytime, not that you need another expert!
10		How do you plan for speaking and listening activities?
		Planning, as such at the moment we haven't got anything formal, so what I tend to do when I plan for the week, when I'm modelling writing or modelling reading, or something like that, I will take a section out of at least two or three mornings, to say, paired work or ask questions about such and such or hot seating, or something along those lines, that's how I put it in my planning. I always try to, because we set up the role play, I always try to get one group, every session, to have a go at the role play, so that every group has a go, because to me it's as important as writing down, so they need the speaking and listening skills, plus they do have writing skills as well because they have to write things down, make list and whatever in the one we're doing now. So, that's how I

	plan it.
11	How do you organise and teach speaking and listening activities?
	Well I organise it... I don't have a specific buddy system, and I don't have a more able and less able child sit together, I tend to have the less able sit with me or sit with my TA anyway, when we are on the carpet doing literacy so, that's what usually happens and she's excellent so she works an awful lot with them, I'm a very lucky woman. And we tend to, I tend to not to get involved when they are pairing up, when they are doing their talking, I listen and I'll ask pertinent questions, to see who actually has done the job and who's doing what they are supposed to do. I was encouraged by our LEA adviser when we had our focus visit to try and write down when they are doing their paired work, but with having a lot of children in this class, who are either still struggling with their writing or are not confident writers, I've not really done a lot of that, I prefer the speaking. **Right, do paired speaking but not paired writing?** Yes, they do have a go, but I like the... we use the post-its, which they like as well, and we do that in science. And I always have a group; I make sure I have got a group every day doing some role play. That's more or less, unless I write down groups or whatever.
12	How do you assess speaking and listening activities?
	Is there anything in addition to what you said earlier? No formal, it's very informal and teacher based and teacher led. I think you have to give us the benefit of the doubt, we are teachers, we are experts at that, we know what we want, and sometimes we slip up but we still know what we want and what we want the children to achieve. **But what happens is you've still got to plan for reading and writing, so by not having any planning for speaking and listening that again applies it has less status.** Yes, that's why we always include it somewhere or other when it's making comments about paired work or hot seating, or something on those lines.
13	What benefits do you believe can come from collaborative work? a) For the staff. b) For the children.
	There's a lot of satisfaction, for me personally, to listen to the children talking to each other and learning, and you can hear them learning. When sometimes they are working independently, and they're getting on with it, you don't know, until you look at their work later, whether they've got what you wanted them to get. But if they're working as a pair or as a group, and you can go round, or you can sit at a table for five minutes or something, you know within an instant, and if you overhear something that they haven't got it you can be over like a shot, or my TAs, and we can sort any problems. **So from the children's point of view again, would you think the same thing about them?** Yes, it gives them confidence. 19:48
14	Do you feel under pressure that every child should record something every lesson?
	No, I'm not that kind of teacher! Not at all! **You are not worried, you don't feel you have got any pressure?** I think with what's happened at our school, and the Ofsted, with us being monitored an awful lot, I think that's put a little bit of pressure on us. I know there was a comment made just after the Ofsted, that maybe my literacy book wasn't as full as it should be, and it wasn't made at me it was somebody else that said it to me who shouldn't have said it, and that hurt me a great deal because I thought that person should know how I work, and they've only got to come in, and they will know exactly how I work. I mean, we've talked about this, I mean, our Literacy Adviser has said the same thing, she said, I have not got a tunnel work in my book and they are in Year 5, we do a lot of discussion, we do a lot on white boards, because these children, because they lack so much in confidence, to write, to speak, encouraged to listen – they are terrible listeners, a lot of it is practical work. You feel the pressure now and again but not a great deal, not a great deal, and with being Year 1, I think, a lot of it is, it's such a practical, practical learning.
15	In what ways do you model speaking and listening? (Compared with how you would in shared reading and shared writing).
	We've had a go at teaching them the role play, getting into character, that's one thing we had to do with specifically with this class because they're very poor. We've had a go with hot seating, where I've either been in the hot seat or my TA has been in the hot seat, or we've been modelling questions.
16	How do you foster and promote paired and group work?
	I think the good thing about paired work is that it's done from the very beginning, it's done in Reception, Year 2, and so our children understand what they have to do. And they have to be reminded when they come up and they go to each class, and they have to be reminded of it, they have to be reminded of the rules, but because three of us all foster, really are interested in it, we do it anyway and so our children know exactly what they are doing. We all have different ideas of what we should do, obviously, as every person has, we all do it differently. **But the ethos is there.** Yes.
17	What types of speaking and listening activities do you use in different curricular areas?
	Right, the likes of the history we do the hot seating, and we do drama, role play, using the

	artefacts. Science, they will often have discussions in groups, not just practical, about things they have to know anyway, science they can have a little chat to each other, we've had a go at KWL grids and they enjoy having a go at those. It's the same thing with geography, it's the same thing with most of the foundation subjects, it's talking to each other, it's knowing what each other knows, it's working together if need be, it's drama if it fits in, it's a little bit of role play if it fits in.	
18	Do you think the Foundation Stage Curriculum and the NLS give enough objectives and support to plan, teach and assess speaking and listening?	
	No! It's not giving the emphasis it deserves and needs, and I think only now, it's very, very junior written, it's all paper, paper, paper. Gets things down, get the assessment, get evidence, whereas I think now people are staring to realise how import speaking and listening is. Some of us have always done it!	
19	Do you think that the year group children are in makes speaking and listening or collaborative work any more important or difficult to teach?	
	I don't think there's any problem in Foundation, maybe Nursery, a little, I think it would be more difficult, but I think Foundation 2 and Key Stage 1, I think, very much, much of a muchness, even up to Year 3. I think after Year 3 it starts to hit with the work, and I think teacher's attitudes change, especially top end of Key Stage 2. I know, my good friend [name withheld] who has not long left here, she was not into it at all, and it wasn't necessarily that she wasn't able to do it because she could do it standing on her head, it was the children, she didn't feel confident enough, and she won't mind me saying that. But I think it does depend very much on the age of the child, and how the teacher feels speaking and listening, how important it is. **Do you think there is any reason why people shouldn't pursue speaking and listening right the way through age groups?** No! It's important. It's a foundation I think of everything, the children love it, they love getting the chance. My kids come in on a Monday morning and we have circle news time. At ten past nine, and sometimes it can go on for hours, I have a little timer, I let them go for a while for the first term or wherever, then I have a timer which is about thirty seconds, twenty five seconds, or I'll go beep! Finish now, pass it on, got Whinny the Pooh... but they've got to, they're desperate, as soon as they come in the morning they've got to tell us their news, and I don't think that... they should be doing that in Year 6. Plus you can talk about things that might be bothering you, you can talk about things that worrying you. I mean, we had a really good session this afternoon in RE, we were talking about differences but we got on to what makes us happy or sad in our family and the differences in our families, and they've all got step brothers, step sisters, half brothers, half sisters, and it was brilliant! And this was ten past one, and we didn't stop talking, they were all sitting at the table, until ten to two, and not one of them was naughty, because we were all interested in what we were listening to and what we were talking about, because I tell them about my home life, they love that!	
20	Do you have any comments that you would like to add about speaking and listening or children working collaboratively?	
	No I don't think so; I think I've more or less covered it.	
	Any supplementary questions used and general comments	
	Do you think the NLS has promoted or prevented speaking and listening and creativity?	
	Prevented! It's work, work, work, work – written work, written work, written work all the time. **Total time 28:58 (12:48 + 16:10)**	

Teacher Interview Questions

Foundation	KS1	Lower KS2 X	Upper KS2

Disk 1 ~ Track 27	
1	Do you think speaking and listening receives less emphasis than reading and writing, and if so, why?
	Well yes, I think it does, and originally I think it was because, it wasn't seen as a separate issue. It was just something that children did, but we didn't really comment upon it. They were just expected to speak, to listen, but we didn't really sort of, see it as something we needed to look into.
2	In your opinion, are there any factors to do with the school or local area that affect children's speaking and listening skills?
	Yeah, I think the way the children react, a lot of that is to do with the way that they are actually spoken to at home. Parents don't seem to spend a lot of time talking to them. I notice, I've been in the infants and I'm in the juniors now, I've noticed that parents would rather put them in front of a television rather than hold a conversation with the children directly. School wise, I think in some ways originally **(interruption).** A lot of the time the children when they come in their speaking and listening skills are very poor, so the school may be behind in it but it because the children do come in at such a low level, so we build up a lot on that, so it's quite difficult.
3	What do you think of the recent box of materials to support speaking and listening?
	Having just received it! I've just had a chance to literally have a quick glance through it, but it does look as though it's going to be useful, as long as we get the training to go along with it, which I think we are. **5.56**
4	Do you have any concerns about the planning, teaching and assessment of speaking and listening and also children working together?
	I haven't got any concerns but, that is as long as the guidance we're given, is clear, so that we know what we are looking for with the children – and actually the children - speaking and listening as part of the lessons I haven't got a problem with at all. I do think it's very important.
5	Do you specifically tell children when they can work together and does this vary according to the lesson?
	I do and I find I tend to do it more when I send them off for a task, I'll say they are going to be working in pairs, working as a group or working individually. It depends again on what I want from the activity, if it needs to be something that they talk about I'll encourage them to talk, if it's something I want them to do, so I know their opinion or what level they're at, I'll ask them to do their work individually.
6	In your opinion, does collaborative work support or hinder task completion?
	I think it depends upon time constraints, because if the children aren't given enough time, to actually carry out that activity then it's not worth them doing it, so as long as they're given the chance to talk before they need to actually complete the work then I find it's alright but if it's sort of a quick thing, it depends upon the length of the task they have got to complete, so whatever you want written down it depends on the length of that as well, so sometimes it can be a hindrance to them, but I think as teachers we've got to be aware of that as well, which would go back to our planning as well, and being aware of what we need to do time wise with the children.
7	Do you think that children can support each other's learning, and if so, in what ways?
	I think they can, in the sense that sometimes you might have a task for the children to do, more able ones can support the less able by talking to them about it and saying you know, this is what we have got to do. Also, that depending on what you are actually doing with the children, whatever lesson it is, children have different ideas about things, so it's not just about ability, it's about their knowledge that they can bring to a lesson. Someone who might be very quiet and you wouldn't expect to be able to say much, might have an important thing that they have experienced outside of school that they can bring to that lesson, so I think that in a lot of ways it can be supportive.
8	Do you feel that children complete their work better when working independently?
	Not necessarily, I find some children lack confidence, in that you will give them instructions and then you can look around the class and you can actually see children, sort of looking at others, 'What am I supposed to do?' 'What am I meant to be doing now?' Whereas if they are working together in a group, there's always a leader, there's somebody who will say right, this is what we're doing, and they will guide, if somebody is not doing what they are supposed to be doing they will say, no that's not what you are supposed to be doing! So in that way, being independent isn't necessarily right for every child.
9	What would be the most effective means in developing your skills in planning, teaching and

	assessing speaking and listening and also promoting collaborative work?
	To see the planning in action. So see an actual lesson where speaking and listening has been planned for, how the teacher has done it and how it's going on in action. And again, the teaching itself, you know, what strategies teachers can use, and to see a teacher doing that assessment as well. So it's really, I'd find it would be better to see another teacher doing it , to work with somebody else rather than trying to just doing it by myself and think well, am I doing it right, rather like the children do. So, yeah, I would find it better to work together, to make sure that I'm doing it right and that I've got the right ideas. I find that actually doing is better; I'll understand it a bit more.
10	How do you plan for speaking and listening activities?
	At present, it's mainly during the lesson I'll sort of say to myself right, I want the children to work together in this one, I might say at that time right, they would actually be better working in a group, I might have said they will work in pairs. But I can see, maybe if it's a science activity, I've got them working in pairs, I might say, actually they might be better working as a group, to get through the work on this. So that's how I would sort of plan for it, not really as a written, at the moment. I know there are within the literacy, there's certain points saying in it speaking and listening opportunities, but as such I've not really focused in, probably because we've not gone through the training. Whereas we are promoting it but, I think that would guide more then, I'd feel more confident about it.
11	How do you organise and teach speaking and listening activities?
	At present I would say that I'm not really aware that I do organise as such, but, again within the lesson I'll be saying to them, this is what you're doing, and this is how you do it. So it might be post planning, after the event, saying children work as – this.
12	How do you assess speaking and listening activities?
	Really at the moment the only assessment that I'm doing is to look at them and to see which children are actually speaking and listening: are there children who are sitting back, not taking part at all no matter what you're doing, or, which children are leading the discussion and are not giving other children opportunities, but again I've not recorded in any way those sorts of results. I don't keep a formal log of such yet. But again I think that's down to a training thing, that would make me sort of say, right here I need jot down these – I do make a mental note and I'll come back later and think, oh I do need to move them because they don't work well together, or they're two very quiet people, they need somebody who's a bit livelier with them really. **14.15**
13	What benefits do you believe can come from collaborative work? a) For the staff. b) For the children.
	I think for the children, they benefit from it because they get experience of other children's ideas, but also, I think it helps build their confidence, that an activity that they might of felt they couldn't do, by working with other children they realise that they can, another child will trigger something off with them and they will say, oh yeah I know how to do that. And for myself personally, I find it's easier to go round when the children are working collaboratively, you've got them talking, whereas when they're working individually you don't know what's going on in their head. Whereas when you can hear them chatting you can pick up on different point and go, Oh! what was that you just said then? And, why was that? And, where did you get that idea? You know, this kind of thing that you can extend their learning their learning as well through it. You know, I've had incidences today where I have asked the children to do something we were doing in numeracy, I asked the children to do something, and I had to go back and say oh hang on a minute, I've got some children who are doing that and some children who are doing that, this is the way I want you to go with it, so that's where it's useful.
14	Do you feel under pressure that every child should record something every lesson?
	I think yes. As juniors you do feel under pressure, I mean I think in the infants as well, there's a certain amount of pressure to have, you know, recordings in books, and I think that's something that we need to look at, that if staff are worried about using speaking and listening, we've got to show that that's what went on in that lesson, to justify, that yes actually, although the children didn't physically record, they were taking part in an activity and they were getting something from it. There's' a mixture of ways isn't there really, I think that depends on staff confidence as well, that people might say well I'm not recording myself taking a lesson, or that kind of thing. **18.00**
15	In what ways do you model speaking and listening? (Compared with how you would in shared reading and shared writing).
	I think, first of all, when the children are taking part in an activity, so it might be, well, it could be just at the start of the lesson when I'm introducing something, I try to model to them, that when a child is answering a question, if I've asked a question or that something I've said has triggered a response from a child, I'll focus on the person talking and really listen to them, and then I'll say to

	other children, did you hear what they said? Where you listening carefully? I try to bring it round but it can be difficult because some children will not automatically listen to others, when they respond to you they'll say, erm Miss, they don't talk to each other. It'll be, well Miss we thought… No, talk to the others. So I try to model and say, well did you hear that Jack, or Joe said this, just to try and get them. So I try and model what I'm doing there. So modelling really is just basically showing that I'm listening to the child and, maybe repeating something that they've said, so it reinforces to the other children that, that point of view, the child's point of view is as important as my point of view.
16	How do you foster and promote paired and group work?
	I'd say, by encouraging them to work together, the class actually now, because we have done a lot of paired and group work, they will say to me, can we work as a group? Can I work with a partner? Or if they're sat by themselves they will go, I haven't got a partner! And I'll say, well you don't need somebody now, or, you can work as a group, you can work as threes if it's one of the smaller tables. So they are, really, because we have worked throughout the year, having a go at in groups and in pairs, which is something I have done since being in the infants, I've tried, because I know at college, we were encouraged, you know, get some group work going, and especially through the literacy it was a lot of group work in the infants. So that would be what? This is seven years teaching, so, for about seven years I've been trying to little bits, but now it's becoming more of an emphasis.
17	What types of speaking and listening activities do you use in different curricular areas?
	I would say at the moment, for the likes of science, it's through practical work. Where the children will talk about an activity they are doing, what they've got to do, how they've got to do it, and they'll be talking to each other about how they're going to set it up, what they're going to use. Then in the likes of history, geography, I find, if they're doing any research it will be, probably more paired work there, and I would have them reading through things and then talking about what they have found out. So, it's that kind of an activity, they are recording, but they're talking about what they have found out, whether they think it is relevant, so, they are about the most ways I use them.
18	Do you think the Foundation Stage Curriculum and the NLS give enough objectives and support to plan, teach and assess speaking and listening?
	Well, I'll just put one word there, NO! Because, if there was enough we'd be doing it, and there would be ideas for us to use that we would feel, we'd have identified it as more of an important issue than the little bit that is just stuck at the end of the objectives sort of saying, oh, you can do this as well. So, the people are more in on, you know, text level, sentence, you know, all this kind of thing rather than that, so, no, they don't. **23.00**
19	Do you think that the year group children are in makes speaking and listening or collaborative work any more important or difficult to teach?
	I think no, because, I was looking at it from the point of view of, if it's taken through the school, so if it's promoted from nursery, right the way through the school then by the time they get to juniors it's not going to be difficult to teach because the children are going to be used to it, they're going to be aware of it so it'll be something they'll take on board automatically. So really at present, I don't think it's any more difficult, you know, people might sort of say well, how about the nursery? How about the receptions class? But I think that the nature of the foundation stages, that's where the most speaking and listening is going to take place because the children are of an age that they've got to tell a teacher, a teaching assistant, what they think because they can't record it, and then as they go through it, it could be the children are thinking will I going to get into trouble if I start talking or whatever. So it's one of those, but I think that there shouldn't be, there really shouldn't be that much difficulty, and that it's important in all the age groups. (you chat). I think that as the teacher you've got to have a strategy. At first, when you start doing it first of all, you've got to make sure that the children have got a clear focus on what you want them to do. So maybe it's at first letting them talk a longer time and then bringing them back and finding out if they've focused on what you've specifically asked, and it might mean stopping them, and saying, hang on a minute, you've gone off there, you really need to focus back, what do I want to know at the end of this? What are you going to tell me at the end of this? So it's bringing it back, and I think if you start that, bits at a time, then children will come back and get used to it, it is of a case of getting used to it. If you give up then you know, it's hard then you've lost that chance of the children working together haven't you?
20	Do you have any comments that you would like to add about speaking and listening or children working collaboratively?
	Well, at the moment I know that as a staff we're trying to promote speaking and listening, and I think with the children in mind over the next twelve months I think we're going to promote it a lot more within as many subjects as we possibly can. We've aware, we've been aware of speaking and listening, maybe, say over the last twelve months, thinking of it literacy wise, but now we're

thinking, well, it is in other subjects, and it's saying, oh yea, they were doing that today, they were doing it here, they were doing it in the maths, they were doing it, and not just saying, right well, we speak and listen in literacy and I don't know what we do in numeracy or anything else! It's one of those. (you talk, teacher responds). They do actually, in fact sometimes I think other subjects are probably better for it, because with literacy we get hung up on the writing and everything else, whereas the likes of the science it is about talking what they're doing, how they're doing it, what they need, that kind of thing. So we might find that the speaking and listening is more other subjects and that we come back to the literacy and we say we have promoted it, but we actually promoted it cross-curricular, rather than just a big heavy emphasis in our literacy, because it could end up as another thing that gets thrown out of the Literacy Hour, right, we are not doing our speaking and listening in the literacy we are going to put that with the spelling or whatever else outside it. **27.50**

Any supplementary questions used and general comments

Do you think the NLS has promoted or prevented speaking and listening and creativity?

I think it can… it depends on how as a staff you are with it, I know where trying to use the strategy but not be hemmed in by it, and I think people are now getting a little more confident about stepping out of those boundaries. I know at the moment, are focus at the moment has been writing, because writing came up as an issue, but that's throughout the country, so, it's one of those, the literacy, I think in some ways it can be as constraining as you want it to be, it's whether or not you feel you can sort of say well hang on, no, we're going to break out a little bit and do things that are little bit different. What we're trying to do at the moment, we've got… we're looking at the role play at the moment and also, what we're trying to do as a staff is, looking at our year, you know all of our different subjects? And looking for ways that we can link those subjects together. So, for example, last term, I was looking at India, and it was amazing how amazing how many different areas I was able to link that into. So that leant itself to an area of having a role play area, to do with India, but I had it in Art, I had it in my IT, so I think that's ways in which we can promote the speaking and listening, looking at the curriculum as a whole for the term or the half-term and say, right, I'm going to promote it, I'm going to do this, this, this and this.

Total time 30:07

Teacher Interview Questions

Foundation	KS1	Lower KS2	Upper KS2 X

Disk 2 ~ Track 5	
1	Do you think speaking and listening receives less emphasis than reading and writing, and if so, why?
	Yes I think it does receive less emphasis. I think basically it's because it's not tested or examined, and Ofsted don't really focus on it too much.
2	In your opinion, are there any factors to do with the school or local area that affect children's speaking and listening skills?
	It think the school, because it's a one form entry, I think perhaps there would be more speaking across the year groups, opportunities to present, do a presentation, an oral presentation to groups, there's still that but I think you work better together in groups, and do more speaking and listening. There's no formal speaking and listening, we don't do any at primary and yet at GCSE they do do a formal speaking and listening piece, but we don't do any and I can't remember what it was called. **(She tries to remember something here)** It was something we used to get tested on when I was at school. It was a specific thing where you had to read a piece or memorise and read it, and it was due with your pronunciation and clear speaking, and that was done when I was at school, and they don't seem to have that formal speaking when you would be tested. I'm not sure what you meant by 'the local area'. **Socio economic, or any particular thing, when you ask somebody a question that it might be typical nationally but in our area it's like this.** Right, I think that obviously because of the area, there's perhaps not as much emphasis on speaking and listening at home, and also there may be, their vocabulary may not be extended when they come into school, so there is an issue there. **2.41**
3	What do you think of the recent box of materials to support speaking and listening?
	I thought it was great, I like the way that they had branched the strands off, and I like the way they gave specific lessons because I think that's what you need, specific lessons to teach speaking and listening skills. I just don't know where it's going to fit in and how we are going to fit it in, I mean, I do lots of speaking and listening, maybe my kids say we don't, but I try to lots of presentations and things like that, things that are specifically geared up so they *have* to speak out, and they have to speak out in front of people. And you can see by just watching that philosophy group then, they find it incredibly difficult to speak, and all I do all the time is to go up and say look at me, don't say Miss, but they are so ingrained on focusing on me and saying 'Miss Miss', and I think part of it is shyness and I think part of it is practice. **3.50**
4	Do you have any concerns about the planning, teaching and assessment of speaking and listening and also children working together?
	Nothing myself for the planning, or the teaching particularly, yes for the assessment, I think it would be much better for me if I had somebody else in the class who knew and was trained how to assess so that I could just do it and they could assess it because assessment is a nightmare really and it's easier to box it off in a test. Getting the assessment is a bit like the Foundation Stage, for me, of assessing things as they are going on and I think that for them it's a nightmare as I think it is for me. The other thing is that when children are working together they may not stay on task, and they didn't did they! **5.00 I think staff are the same when you go on courses, you stay on task for a bit and then you come back to it, children are only mimicking what we do** Yes, what comes naturally, **It's only that we are more aware of it that we should be on task all the time... there are times when we drift off but come back again.** And do you think they have that discipline to come back again? We tend to enforce that discipline, maybe that would come naturally, perhaps you need that little reminder, ok, you've got 5 minutes to finish this off for whatever, but you need to be back on task. **I don't think it's as disastrous as it could be, they might need a reminder.** I love to do it but I seem to have this nagging thing going that that group are talking about football from last night and how much are we actually getting dome here. That's why I did the philosophy because I thought it was very controlled in a way, because everyone is listening to everyone else and yet it's meant to come from them, hopefully the idea is that I would step out of the situation and they would be doing the debate entirely on their own. But because it's in a big group, they have to wait, you see in a small group you get more chance to speak don't you. **As far as assessment I think it has to be ongoing focusing on one or two children, making a few notes, then making sure you've gone through all of them, not a few ticks but making certain comments in particular areas, but not feeling they all have to be done at the same time.** The one that we are using, or supposed to be using, the files are all in the cupboard because we were supposed to have the Inservice day on speaking and listening but that didn't

materialise…it's the Australian one, the speaking and listening…I can't remember the book but it's the progression in Speaking and listening, you do have the tick boxes in the same way, but because it's not too specific I think, it's more generic and it's also more progressive so you've got a few sheets, I think it's more helpful, especially for writing notes down, I think that's really helpful to write notes down, but I'm really bad at it! **You can have prompt sheets, like, is able to challenge, sustain an argument, is able to listen and respond, so you can make a couple of notes and keep them ring bound.** That's what it's like, I'll show you later, but we just… the boxes aren't big enough to make notes but there are comments at the end that we can make, I tend to just go through at the end of the year, or when I have to fill those boxes in, and say, ok, let me think back, but your memory is fallible isn't it. **I think if you take a couple of children in the week, you don't have to assess them all on the same activity, it could be in Science, History or Geography, looking at expressing opinion, asking for explanation, giving more detail, it can just be part of any activity that's going on.** I think because I do lots of speaking and listening, I do specific things, 'ok, you're now going to present a piece about earth and space… you're going to have to present it in assembly.' Then I get a lot of opportunity to see, I tend to keep doing those sorts of things of working with groups, and allowing them to fail, and if they fail they've got to present it in that poor fashion, they will start to see that they want to keep on task, that they don't want to work with that group because they mess about and I want to get on. Over the year you start to see that when you tell them to do a certain task, and give them a certain length of time, they get it done and they are going to present it in front of other people. And perhaps it's a little bit of bullying! It has got a purpose and I think they know what they should do because they are getting it modelled as a group of children that do it well, they see and we talk about why that was a better presentation, what was good about it, what to do to make theirs more successful. But I found a book, a really good book on speaking and listening but it was for secondary school, so we would have to adapt it, but I thought if we had something like that, for all the different strands, different ideas and different activities, which I know that box is meant to be covering, but it's just too much, isn't it, too thick and heavy and wordy **I think you just need to make sure that every half tem you try out something.** we were just going to do one strand, it said you can just start off… drama was the best one to start off with something, and we were supposed to do it this term and I feel bad because I haven't developed the things for speaking and listening, because I'm very keen but other things cram in, and it gets sidelined. I think because it's something that develops, and because it's something that has a knock-on effect, it's not quantifiable, in that you can't say ok, I can see that I've done that and therefore this has happened. I can see where it's working, but it just takes a while to develop, you don't see that instant effect, perhaps it isn't, it will take a long time to develop, and it will be one to show Ofsted something, one to show that we've got something, we're doing something, there's the paperwork, there is it all, and speaking and listening is not like that, it's something that's a drip effect. **12.00**

5	Do you specifically tell children when they can work together and does this vary according to the lesson?
	No, they just assume that they can work together because I encourage it all the time. That's one of the things I talk about right at the beginning, when children say 'He's copying me!', but if he is that's good! He's using his initiative. So I encourage them to, not copy as in I'll write it down so you can write it with me, you do get that don't you. I encourage the supporting of other children, so they assume they can work together but they still shout out, 'Miss can we work together?', and I think what they mean by that is can we do the same piece of work, because usually I'll say to them, when I want one separate piece of work they can work collaboratively, or they can work collaboratively and have the same piece of work. For poetry I might say, ok, you can make up a poem working together, for something like research on a topic I'll say you can work together or if you're writing a story you can work together, you can have some ideas but I want you to have your own writing, and you work as a response partner to each other. **Do you ever say I want you to work in pairs for this or groups for this?** Yes, it depends upon, sometimes I want you to works in fours, or I'll put them in pairs, or very occasionally I'll say friendship groups. **13.45**
6	In your opinion, does collaborative work support or hinder task completion?
	It supports, but in certain groups it may hinder, but I found, as I say, they find out the consequences of that hindering themselves.
7	Do you think that children can support each other's learning, and if so, in what ways?
	Yes, I think they can give advice and give ideas, they can give encouragement. Learning is a process and they may make mistakes, and I'll tell them when they've got it wrong. And they'll go 'Oh no', but I'll say its fine, and you will learn, what they have learned together, talk together, what they have found out, that's why I like philosophy because there's no right or wrong, it's just discovering and thinking **So do you do that regularly?** Yes, I've only just started it.
8	Do you feel that children complete their work better when working independently?

	Sometimes yes, because I will send children out if I notice that they're chatting a lot and not getting on, and I expect them to do more, I'll just say 'would you like to work outside?', and some of them will come to me to ask if they can work outside and they do that a lot actually. They will come up and say it's too noisy in here. Hilda is one of the ones I send out to you, she does actually like to work on her own, I could have sent Stan. There is a few of them that like to work on their own a lot and there's others that are just in the mood for it, so I like to accommodate that if they want to work independently, or if I think they're messing they can go and work outside and they will come back in and will have completed it in 5 minutes and everyone else is behind! Can I have 21 separate classrooms please!
9	What would be the most effective means in developing your skills in planning, teaching and assessing speaking and listening and also promoting collaborative work?
	You cram a lot in your questions, I'm glad I've got it in front of me! I think watching others teach would be a good thing, watching others developing speaking and listening in their class, seeing other people's plans, and having help in the classroom. **Do you mean help like with TA's?** I wouldn't mind another teacher to come in and team teach and that sort of thing. But yes, a TA, I haven't had a TA this year and noticed that there were certain things that I hadn't done as much of as I'd liked to do. I don't know whether it's because when you have another year group you get to a certain pattern of the way of working so, because you've got that help, but when you don't have that help you drop that pattern or change the pattern, I don't what happens **So you don't have a TA in every class here?** No, it's just this class that doesn't have a TA. **That's unlucky.** They have got three less than the other classes so three less means you don't get any! **Can't they split it?** That's what they were going to do at the beginning but it just didn't work like that. I think the idea was that there would be three classroom assistants working between the four classes. But the classroom assistants liked to be, liked to know that they were with a particular class, and they find it difficult to be homeless as it were, and if it was two between four I think it would have worked better, perhaps, I'm not sure, but because historically this class had not received a classroom assistant last year, it was easier just... **Was it just this class?** Because there is 21 **Was it because this group was without one?** Yes, so it will be interesting to see how they develop and how the classes have developed. I mean, there are 29 in Year 6 and you would expect someone especially in Year 6 anyway, but then in Year... it's 24 and 24 or is it 24 and 26, anyway it's not that many considering you've got no help at all. **18.45** But I think in Year 3 you need them for the readers and things like that, but I had this class in year three and we used to just stay in at playtime and do the reading. Luckily they were just a bright class and just got a few that were special needs.
10	How do you plan for speaking and listening activities?
	I had to think, what do I do, how do I plan it. And I look at the outcome, what do I want this particular week, what do I want them to achieve this week, and if I've got a presentation for them to do then we'll work specifically towards that, so I might get them doing the research first or whatever, and then getting into groups and they really direct the work from then on, and I will work with the less able and the rest of the groups are just left to find out for themselves, and as I say, they've been given a time limit and have to be sensible. It might be a play, they might be doing a role play, and I notice that they can do it so easily from the book now, they just pick up a book and read their speaking parts form the book, with saying 'you said, he said', and that's probably because they have done a lot of that, but they do tend to like their little scripts and they now read from their scripts. . . 'You haven't' got time, you'll have to adlib it, you've got to improvise... so they can do that, but they do stuff like that but it is this presenting in front of class and they spend a lot of time doing that, but how do I plan. **So do you just write it in?** Yes I do, but then I'll do a lot of ad hoc things, I mean off the cuff because maybe I don't think they want to see a lot of speaking and listing throughout this lesson. Perhaps one lesson or maybe two lessons are expected, so I will squeeze other things in that is not in my planning.
11	How do you organise and teach speaking and listening activities?
	I what sense? **You've said that really, that you get them into groups and they direct themselves, and I think you said before about assessment.** I think it depends upon the task, how do I organise it and how do I assess it; I just try to keep it all in my head! And do it in retrospect, which is not good I suppose. **You talk about making notes at the time rather than having to recall info, such as for reports.** Because I do so much I have always got a memory, a very clear memory of how they've come along, and also because I'm thinking, everybody needs extra speaking and listening, you can not have too much I don't think, and so, I don't think I would say I'd have to work specifically with that group to build up this, this or this, but I'm building up everyone's all together and I'm doing the modelling, and not only encourage them I do force them, I do force them, so we have everybody speaking and they read out a lot and use their voices. **I suppose from assessment you have something written down so you can make a target for the children to have, so they can have their own targets.** Yes, that would be helpful, and I've

	found it's helpful with the reading particularly, they really increased their scores on reading, because we went over to give them specific targets. I don't know what happened with the writing, that seemed to, capital letters and punctuation stuff went completely out of the window, and it's much harder to give targets to those kind of activities unless it's specific to that task. You are now going to write a story and your targets for story writing are. And I think it's the same with speaking and listening, it might be, ok you're going to do, and I keep coming back to this oral presentation, I think that really gives them the confidence if they have to speak and they have to organise their work and they have to present it in front of an audience. I think anything will develop from that. So when they speak in a little group they'll have that confidence I think. And then we do it with classroom things, people will listen to each other, philosophy tends to cover that side.
12	How do you assess speaking and listening activities?
	See above.
13	What benefits do you believe can come from collaborative work? a) For the staff. b) For the children.
	I think guidance, encouragement and support, so if you're working with one group then you know that another group is getting the guidance and support and I've heard them keeping each other on task when they're working together, 'Come on we've got to finish this', that means I can work with one group because of that so I think for the teacher it's good. And for the children, again, it's that guidance, support and encouragement. **26.00**
14	Do you feel under pressure that every child should record something every lesson?
	I've said no straight away, defiantly not every lesson. Sometimes I'll think, oh! I've done too much speaking and listening this week! So, better get something in their books especially because we've got a particular problem with writing. But I think speaking and listening feeds the writing but it's only and intuitive thing and I haven't... because I've only been teaching four years, this is my fourth year, I haven't seen so much evidence, I'm only assuming that evidence is there. Then when you look at the writing, horror of horrors oh no! **It's difficult, good writing I think has got to come from good speaking and listening.** It's the punctuation that you don't cover you see, I mean, you loose so many marks form punctuation so definitely the ideas are there and the confidence.
15	In what ways do you model speaking and listening? (Compared with how you would in shared reading and shared writing).
	I probably don't! I model writing and I model reading, and I'm thinking, do I model speaking and listening? I probably don't I probably don't give it as much attention that's food for thought that is really, for me. Because I'd have to have another teacher there to be modelling it with and I know on that tape it does show another teacher doesn't it, if it's the right tape I'm thinking of, where they are showing that modelling with another teacher, and as far as presentation goes I don't think I've stood up there and said, 'This is the way you can do it', I think I've just allowed them to! **(Pause)** I think that's what they did on this tape, they brought a poor speaker in, one of the teachers was mumbling and the children picking up incidences of what they could improve, rather than doing it with another child, they were saying, 'don't do it with other children', yet I do. I model reading out, so change in my voice and things like that, and I model the drama, and I'm thinking do I model the presentation. It was a while ago, I think I'd have to se myself in action, step back, and say, 'you are modelling this', but I don't know. (You go into lengthy conversation about modelling – that people might not consciously be aware of it) **30.00** That's bad modelling, I say everyone look at this person but I'm not going to! It's a bit weird! I'm just thinking now, I do correct pronunciation as well, that's not modelling.
16	How do you foster and promote paired and group work?
	I encourage it verbally, and I have given them response partner material, so if they are working on a story, or a piece of non-fiction, they'll have a script to work to which they will be checking each others work. I suppose I encourage it by giving them one sheet of paper, or one book, so one will scribe or they will both write on the same piece of paper. I quite often give them a big sheet of paper and say, you can add to this one piece and then present it. So, with group work, I will say, you will have to present something as a group and everyone will need to speak, and you will have to work out who is going to do what. And with paired, if they are doing a drama piece, any group work or paired work it's got to be shared. For say a poem, if they are writing a poem together they'll read it together, or read one line each or be the speaking or whatever. **33.28**
17	What types of speaking and listening activities do you use in different curricular areas?
	I use hot seating in History, or drama, we use quite a lot of discussion and drama in RE, and Philosophy. Because they are always working together I suppose it could be in Maths again where they are working out a problem together, in a pair, and then they will present their findings as well, and they will use the board, where the children's work is presented underneath, or on sheets, and

		they will have to present it at the front.
18	Do you think the Foundation Stage Curriculum and the NLS give enough objectives and support to plan, teach and assess speaking and listening?	
	Yes I think they do give enough objectives… perhaps not enough for presentation, they just tend to give some ideas of what you can do, certainly for each unit there are speaking and listening suggestions, so you tend to get, these are the written outcomes we want, these are their suggestions for speaking a listening so you can sort of take them or leave them, perhaps they need to be more prescriptive. I think they probably need to do more about presentation, I am all for this formal addressing of an audience. **35.50**	
19	Do you think that the year group children are in makes speaking and listening or collaborative work any more important or difficult to teach?	
	I think its important right throughout. But I know there's more of a focus in Foundation and then it gets less and less as time goes on, and by Year 6 they should be eloquent and be speaking and presenting and do all of this but they don't because that gets squeezed out, and the more and more writing they have to do. But I think its possibly more difficult to teach if it hasn't been embedded earlier, it's very difficult to get it in by Year 5 and Year 6 if they haven't had much experience of this and their development is poor.	
20	Do you have any comments that you would like to add about speaking and listening or children working collaboratively?	
	No.	

Any supplementary questions used and general comments
Do you think all staff are aware of the Foundation Stage Curriculum and how that's changed perhaps?
No.
Do you think the Foundation Stage and the NLS has promoted or prevented speaking and listening?
In the Foundation Stage no, certainly for the assessment of what they are expecting in the EAZ, put a lot of pressure on assessment of writing, and I guess that will squeeze our speaking and listening. I know when J--- M--- came she was talking about this… I can't remember what she called it, it's very like a philosophical discussion this, very much like encouraging the child and the open ended question, and talking together, I know that's promoted in Foundation Stage, but when the nursery teacher came to me she said we have haven't got anything, we haven't got this pack you've got, it's just for KS1 and KS2, and yet throughout the Foundation Unit plans, which we follow the unit plans, it's very much to so with the speaking, but, there does seem to be this move between taking more speaking into Year 1 and bringing the writing down into Nursery, and we've felt this like two wave effects going on in opposite directions and I don't know where I stand! **Do you think the NLS has promoted or prevented speaking and listening?** I think because it's so packed, it was an add on after they had done pilot unit plans, 'Oh, wait a minute, someone's forgotten speaking and listening!', ok, you can not then go ok, this is really important now, it's all about evidence, the written evidence, and handwriting was a particular issue in our school, and so you think if we are spending lots of time doing oral work, how are they getting the practice of writing. I don't know how to do it, I just think there's probably less and less talk going on at home, less and less writing going on at home, how do we get all of that in as well as teach them a mass of knowledge that they're meant to know. I was doing something, what was is… oh plants, just labelling a plant part, flower parts… carpel, stigma, style… I did that in probably third year seniors, how come we are doing it in year five, juniors you know. There's too much vocabulary, unnecessary vocabulary, and they can't understand just simple words, were cramming them with all this technical vocabulary. They say that the mass of knowledge is increasing so much that there's no way we can get more in, what we really need to teach them is how to do that research, how to think and find out these things themselves, which you do do through collaborative work and do through speaking and listening! But then of course you've still got the written stuff, but I think with all this text speak and female speak, I think it'll only be in school that you will be writing, this will be so alien to everybody else when they go out and write in the world. Who writes formal letters these days, very few.
The last point I need to ask you about Speaking and Literacy, in terms of you being the coordinator, how you feel where the school up to, what needs to happen next, those general issues, and whether you feel you're fully supported when trying to do things?
I think that the point I made before, you can see that I am very supportive of speaking and listening, but because we have this idea that we have this problem with the writing and handwriting, that we've had to address that, and it has to show quickly, so to do speaking and listening… I'm doing a lot this year but I may not if we've got Ofsted next year, I may do more writing, I'm not sure how I'll do this, but I may need more written work in books, and yet, depending what team you get…oh I don't know… but I felt it was a very definite need in the school, that we needed to, and most of the teachers think the same, in

fact all of them, because its… Foundation and KS1 are always coming in and saying 'The children can't speak properly, they don't know how to pronounce words', so I've known it's been a particular issue, and yet when HMI came in I said that to him, and I said we're trying to get onto that talking partners thing, trying to get some training, and he said you seem to rely a lot on training don't you, and he said, and there isn't a particular issue on speaking and listening, I've spoken to the children in the Nursery and I don't think there is. So I was sort of thrown back a bit by that response, thinking maybe I've not go so much of a handle on what's going on, but I thought no, you just know don't you, you just know by what you are getting by Year 3, 4 or 5 that they haven't got that vocabulary, that they haven't got that experience of speaking in a formal manner. And then…the writing issue, yeah… I think you cannot, however much speaking and listening you do, you really can't cover handwriting without doing handwriting, without writing, and so you've got to have the motor skills, and so we've got we've got to practice that and that seems to be a particular issue as well, that the children haven't got those motor skills. **I give examples.** Yes, I think the talking partners thing will hopefully, when we go on that course, will have something specific to give everybody back, so to try out a session to develop things. I think the response which I know is happening in KS1, Foundation and Reception, and that need to be developed possibly more in the Juniors, that will carry on because once you've set that good foundation it's such a shame not to develop that further, and get more sophisticated response by the time they're in Year 6, so they're almost marking their own work, they're critical of each others work in a positive way, then they can almost then mark to a particular criteria, so that's what I hope I would be hoping to develop.
Total time 46:25

Children Interview Questions

Foundation X	KS1	Lower KS2	Upper KS2

Disk 2 ~ Track 4	
1	How often do you work on your own?
6	I do! I work on my own. I work and work and work. I don't have a friend every day. If they do help me I say go away because I don't need help. They think I need help but I don't.
	I work with somebody else because I'm scared on my own.
1	I work with a friend every day.
2	I work in a group with everyone.
3	I work with two people. **Do you ever work on your own without any help?**
4	I work with a friend. **Do you ever work on your own?** Sometimes, two or three times a week.
5	I work on my own. **When, how often do you work on your own?** Every day.
	I work with my friend in a group, two children. **Do you ever work on your own?** No.
7	
8	
2	How often do you work with one friend?
1	Less than once a week.
5	Less than once a week.
2	Every day.
3	I work, I play with Jack.
4	I work with my friends all the time.
7	I work with my friends every day.
6	Every day. **(One person missing, gone to the toilet)**
3	How often do you work in groups?
8	Every day.
7	Every day.
6	I don't work with a friend at all.
5	I work with a friend **This is a group, not one friend.** Every day.
4	Every day.
3	Every day.
2	Once or twice a day.
1	I want to be on my own.
4	What kind of things you do in school with speaking and listening, where you don't have to write anything down, where you talk and listen.
3	Just listen. **What do you listen to?** Listen if you shout out before you read it.
4	Listen to what they say. **What kind of things?**
8	Listen to what they say – shout out – listen to the reading.
	What kind of things do you talk about?
	No reply.
5	What do you like about being able to talk to your friends in school?
7	Playing with each other.
4	Miss, we read this story in our class.
5	I like talking to my friends **Why? What sort of things?** Because they are my friends. **How does it help you?**
6	Is there anything you don't like about speaking and listening?
4	I don't like listening to them and I don't like talking to them, because they give me a headache. Some people give me a headache when they talk too loud to me.
5	They give you a headache because they shout down your ear.
3	
7	Tell me if you prefer - reading, writing or speaking and listening? **11:45**
	4 prefer reading.
	2 prefer writing.
	1 or 2 prefer speaking and listening. **Is it short because one has a loo break?**
2	I like playing if someone plays with me or I play by myself.
4	I like reading and getting on with my books.
8	Is it more difficult to work on your own than with a friend?
	3 yes's.
9	What are the things you like or don't like about working on your own?
5	When I don't know what to do I ask a friend.

6	Because he is all by himself and he has no one to work with and it's really scary. **(Referring to 8's mumble).**
8	You don't know what to do.
10	What is good or bad about working with other children?
3	I like playing with them and I like...
1	I don't like it when they talk.
2	When he plays with me, I want to play with a different friend.
11	How can you help your friends in class, how can they help you?
5	Because they work with me and they talk to me.
7	They tell yer and help yer.
2	When I go on the floor I take turns with Jack.
1	**(says something very quiet about a door being locked)**
12	If you get stuck on your work, do you ask the teacher or a friend? **22:00**
4	My friend... or my teacher.
3	I would ask a friend.
2	I would ask the teacher.
5	I would ask my friend because I help her with my work everyday.
4	I would ask just my friend. **(pause)** And my teacher.
7	I would ask my teacher and my friend.
8	I would ask my friend and my teacher.
6	Friend! No, not the teacher.
13	When people are talking how can you show you are listening?
5	I'm listening to when they are reading and I'm listening to them when they are talking and to when they are singing. **How can they tell you have been listening?** Because I'm looking at them. **Brilliant... that's really good.**
4	If I'm listening to people, and then they come and look at me when I'm talking to a person, I will want to talk to them, they are my best friend.
14	If you are working in a group with other people how can you make sure it goes well? 27:00
2	Because they are my best friend and I love them so much.
3	I... I like them and I play with them every day.
1	When I am outside playing football, I always get the ball far away.
5	If I have a friend and I'm outside playing with them I went in then went back outside.
15	If you have to work with someone would you like to choose yourself or are you happy for the teacher to choose?
7	The teacher chooses.
6	What about it if I'm playing with someone and then they 'fell' me over, what about if I cry and I just go again. **(Recap question).** I would choose what to do. **Hands up if you prefer to choose your own friends to work with.** 6 choose.
16	Is there any difference between working with one friend or lots of friends? **30:50**
5	I think with lots of friends.
	(Recap question – no response, talking about other things)
1	When I'm playing in a car and another is playing in a car I don't like it when they crash into me. **Total Time 33:00**

Children Interview Questions

Foundation	KS1 X	Lower KS2	Upper KS2

Disk 1 ~ Track 26	
1	How often do you work on your own?
8	We always work on our own, sometimes we work in pairs
7	Or groups.
	Just think about it. Do you work on your own in every lesson?
2	Yeah.
3	Every day.
7	Three times a week.
1	Once a week.
7	Every day.
8	Every day.
5	Every day.
4	Two or three times a week.
2	Every day.
2	How often do you work with one friend?
1	Sometimes.
2	Sometimes.
	How often? You need to give a clearer answer.
1	Less than once a week.
2	Less than once a week.
3	Less.
4	Less.
5	Less.
6	Less.
7	Less.
8	Less.
	So you think a week goes by and you can't work with another person?
8	Yeah, we don't always work in pairs.
3	How often do you work in groups?
5	Every day.
6	I think it's once a week.
	(Repeat the question).
1	Every day.
2	Every day.
3	Twice a week.
4	Two or three times in a week.
5	Once a week.
6	Every day.
7	Every day.
8	Less than once a week.
4	What kind of things you do in school with speaking and listening, where you don't have to write anything down, where you talk and listen.
6	I think it's just less than once a week.
	No, it's not a time now – what things do you do in class that's to do with speaking and listening?
1	We talk about stuff.
5	We tell our teachers stuff about speaking and listening.
	What about thing you talk to other children about?
3	Sometimes miss is telling us about something and we work in pairs or something like that. Sometimes when you are doing stuff you have to talk to your partner, the person next to you.
7	We've got writing partners and Miss tells us to… when we've got to work we've got to work with our writing partner.
8	Miss knows that because that's what we were doing when she came (referring to you).
5	We were doing work when you came to see us in Year one and we were listening to the fire station, and when we finished working about it you went into Year two.
	Can you think of anything else when you talk to people?
3	You talk to our partner and say how do you do the answer and that.

5	What do you like about being able to talk to your friends in school?
1	I like talking about toys and that.
2	(agrees)
5	I like talking about what you do at weekends.
3	Sometimes when were working we've been noisy and Miss shouts for us to be quiet but sometimes when she's in the office she can hear us or in the hall.
6	We have circle time and we can tell news, what we did at the weekend.
6	Is there anything you don't like about speaking and listening?
4	I hate sitting on the carpet because Miss talks too much and you have to listen to work. I don't like people shouting and that and stuff.
3	I was going to say that.
5	You get hot... when miss is talking to you, you get hotter and hotter and hotter.
6	I don't like it when it's too noisy.
4	I hate it when people shout in our class.
8	I hate it when people are talking over other people's voices.
3	Someone is talking quiet and they are talking properly...
7	When I'm doing my work and someone's distracting me.
6	
7	Tell me if you prefer - reading, writing or speaking and listening? **11:40**
	5 prefer reading. 3 prefer writing. **So no one for speaking and listening?** **So what do you prefer about reading?**
5	Its nice stories and I like stories.
7	When you play and you read a story you are down. (Don't understand this).
6	It does let you down. **Why do you like writing the best?**
1	Its good writing about stuff.
3	You can't understand it.
5	And you don't understand what you've writ.
8	Is it more difficult to work on your own than with a friend? **13:50**
4	On yer own.
3	On yer own because you don't get distracted.
6	You don't get distracted – everyone comes over to you. **Stop. Now start again as it's unclear who is saying what. Is it more difficult working on your own? We'll start this end, this time.**
8	Yes.
7	Yes.
6	Yes.
5	Yes
4	No.
3	Yes
2	No.
1	Yes. **So what makes it more difficult?**
7	When you are on your own it's quieter but when you are with your partner you talk a lot to them. When you work on your own someone comes over and says that's wrong this is wrong like that...
6	and it'll annoy yer.
9	What are the things you like or don't like about working on your own?
8	It's more hard because when you do your work... if you don't understand it you get confused and you just don't know what to do. When you work on your own you can't think enough...you need two people so to think about all that stuff, there's plenty to think about. I don't like working on my own.
1	Because it's boring.
3	Sometimes I like it on my own because I get a sentence more longer.
2	I like working on my own. **Why?** Because you can get it done quicker.
10	What is good or bad about working with other children?
	Can anyone think why it is good to work with another person?
6	If you get stuck you can ask the other person.
2	If you can't spell something the other person can help yer.
11	How can you help your friends in class, how can they help you? **19:50**
2	Be good and that and try... and... she will be so excited and that.

8	The person who is your partner you can help them if they are stuck on anything.
7	If there was a word and you don't know what it was you can ask the person next to yer... your friend.
6	If you were working in a pair, doing sums, and you didn't know what 20 add 100 was when it's 120, you could just take the zeros off... so it will make 2 and 10. **Who will do this?** Your partner will have to do it for you.
3	If they are crying you can look after them.
4	If they need help if they fell and that, you can pick them up and carry them to Miss.
1	If someone hasn't got anyone to play with we can go over and play with them.
7	Our friends can help us.
1	Our partners...when you are in partners you can help your partner... you need to talk to each
2	other, talk about how to spell 'shop' and that. Do you know how to spell 'shop'?
6	If you are stuck on something you can go, are you alright, do you need some help, and you can
8	say yes because you are stuck. If you are stuck on a sum they can tell you what the answer is.
4	**But, not about telling you the answer, can they help you work it out?** Yes. **Wouldn't that be more useful?**
5	Yes. **But how could you work it out for yourselves?**
6	If you don't count it in your head, if you don't work it out in your head or your fingers, or if you just
3	guess and just put the number on, you might just get it wrong, but if you do it in your head or your fingers you will be able to do it, in your head or on your fingers you'll be done.
12	If you get stuck on your work, do you ask the teacher or a friend? **25:15**
1	Teacher
2	Friend
4	Teacher
8	Friend.
6	Teacher.
7	Both.
5	Teacher
3	Friend. **Why would you prefer to ask your friend?**
7	Because your friend might be able to give you the answer, but Miss can't can she?
4	Because they could help you work it out and they could... **Why would you prefer to ask the teacher?**
6	Because the teacher is telling yer, she tells you what to do in your work and when to do your work and she knows what to do in the work because she chooses the work. Because the teacher can tell you when you have done your work and the other person can't.
4	**Why ask a friend?** Because they might know the answer and if the friend doesn't know you'll have to ask the teacher.
3	You can ask them (teacher) because they will know the right answer.
13	When people are talking how can you show you are listening?
3	If you are being quiet you can hear.
6	You're looking at them and you are listening.
3	You're staring at them... at circle time your sometimes... you are asked to listen to the sentence what you say.
8	You're just listening to the person, what they are saying, that's because we are doing about speaking and listening. **How does a person know you are listening?**
2	If you are quiet the person knows that you are listening.
7	Just be quiet.
5	I forget.
2	When you're trying to be good when someone is talking to yer, if Miss was talking to me now when I'm just trying to be sensible, I would just ignore him.
14	If you are working in a group with other people how can you make sure it goes well? **31:00**
8	I'm listening to other people's ideas.
2	If you are doing a card or something people will help you and tell you what to do, that would be good... if you don't know you can talk to the other person.
7	Because you can have turns.
2	I like it because if someone is talking to you they can give you good ideas if you have not got ideas you can ask a different person.
5	If I was talking now and I had something good and the teacher asked someone else a silly question then she would have to ask someone else.

2	I know someone who said you're stupid Miss but no one will say that because you will just get shouted at by Miss.
15	If you have to work with someone would you like to choose yourself or are you happy for the teacher to choose?
6	No, I don't choose I just ask the teacher if she can choose someone.
8	Miss, ages ago we done work and we got to pick partners, Miss had to get a piece of paper and put our names down and so we knew our partners, so we would always work with the partner on the piece of paper.
7	I think it's better when you pick it yourself because if you are not clever and the other person is not clever and you are both working together you can't work out what it is. When you work with a partner its better.
16	Is there any difference between working with one friend or lots of friends? **30:50**
	No response! **Let's think about what we said in the first question. How often do you work on your own? 1 person said every single lesson. 5 people said every day. 1 person said two or three times a week. 1 person said once a week. *(children agreed)* How often do you work in pairs? All of you said that you can go less than once a week that means you can for a whole week without working with a partner – is that right?**
3	Yes
6	It could be a month.
	So it could be a month? You don't work in pairs very often then?
3	No.
	You said you work in groups. Four of you said you work in groups every day. Two of you said two or three times a week, one of you said once a week and one said less than once a week. So what you are telling me is that you work more as a group than just the two of you?
All	Yes.
	But most of the time you work on your own, without any help?
All	Yes.
	Total time 38:05

Children Interview Questions

Foundation	KS1	**Lower KS2 X**	Upper KS2

Disk 1 ~ Track 28	
1	How often do you work on your own?
1	Every day.
2	Every day.
3	Every day.
4	Every day.
5	Every day.
6	Two or three times a week.
7	Two or three times a week.
8	Two or three times a week.
2	How often do you work in pairs?
1	Less than once a week.
2	Two or three times a week.
3	Less than once a week.
4	Two or three times a week.
5	Two or three times a week.
6	Once a week.
7	Once a week.
8	Two or three times a week.
3	How often do you work in groups?
1	Less than once a week.
2	Two or three times a week.
3	Two or three times a week.
4	Less than once a week.
5	Less than once a week.
6	Two or three times a week.
7	Once a week.
8	Once a week.
4	What kind of things you do in school with speaking and listening, where you don't have to write anything down, where you talk and listen.
1	Geography.
2	History.
5	Science.
7	Literacy.
3	Maths.
8	Literacy, ? and dilemmas.
4	Science.
3	Numeracy.
6	Maths, because you can learn about shapes.
5	What do you like about being able to talk to your friends in school?
6	You get to speak what you think.
8	You learn more about what the subject is.
5	You learn more off other people.
7	Sharing ideas.
6	Is there anything you don't like about speaking and listening?
4	When I start doing my work they always start chatting, always start talking when I'm trying to do my work.
8	People are shouting out when I'm trying to answer questions.
6	Sometimes they don't listen to yer.
1	You don't get to write anything up.
7	They're messing when you are listening in the lesson.
3	Miss, when ever you are trying to do your work somebody on our table is talking to you asking what the answer is. (agreed by another).
5	When you are trying to listen to the teacher someone will distract you and tell you something. I can't enjoy it.
2	**If you are not writing do you feel you are not doing work?**
	I like writing.

145

7	Tell me if you prefer - reading, writing or speaking and listening? **7:40**
1	Writing.
2	Reading
3	Reading
4	Reading.
5	Reading.
6	Writing.
7	Reading.
8	Writing.
	Nobody prefers speaking and listening, any particular reason?
All	No.
	Any particular reason? What is it that you prefer reading or writing?
7	I prefer reading because you are writing and reading as well. You are still reading but you don't have to use your hands.
3	I like reading because sometimes you can learn.
1	I like writing because... I just like writing!
8	Is it more difficult to work on your own than with a friend? **13:50**
1	No.
2	No.
3	No.
4	No.
5	It's harder working on your own.
6	No.
7	No.
8	No.
	Why do you prefer working on your own?
1	Because you can put your own answers to the questions down.
2	Because you can work faster.
3	It's better working on your own because if there's anyone with you they might copy your answers. You can get the work done by yourself.
4	It's better because you need to learn it yourself and you don't need other people to help yer.
6	They mess around and sometimes you do it wrong.
	If you work on your own they don't help yer.
2	If you work on your own... if you work with someone else they are always leaning over you and
4	you can't breathe, right in front of you.
3	I like working on my own because, if you're trying to tell them something that you've written down, they are not listening when you are talking about something.
8	I think you should work on your own, you might think of one answer and the other person might think of another and you might go with the other person's answer and get it wrong.
7	
9	What are the things you like or don't like about working on your own?
	You have almost covered this as you have talked about those things. Has anyone got anything else they would like to say about working on their own? Does anyone not like working on their own? (5 respond). What makes it good working with other people? 13:00
5	Because I like working in a pair, it's easier than working on your own, but if you like working in a group it is too noisy. **(Refers to next question as pointed out earlier).**
10	What is good or bad about working with other children?
2	I don't like working with someone else because they distract you.
1	I don't like working on my own because they can start messing with yer and make you not do it and leave your work out.
5	They might make you do wrong answers.
3	I like working on my own because they could start talking to you about something else.
	What about the difference between working in pairs/groups? The advantages/ disadvantages?
6	I think a group because you can write your ideas down and get it done easier with a group... you can get loads of ideas.
4	Pairs... in groups it's all shouting and you can't get on, when you are trying to do something with them they won't do it.
2	I prefer pairs because in a group some will go faster and when you are meant to be working with each other they won't work with yer.
6	I prefer to work in a group because if you are working with partners and trying to talk to yer and the teacher shouts, they get you into trouble because the teacher shouts at you as well.

8	I like working in a pair because when you are in a group and you're trying to say the answer or something they are like shouting at yer and not listening to yer.
	I like working in a pair because in a group some of them don't get on with there work.
11	How can you help your friends in class, how can they help you? **17:15**
1	By talking to them.
7	Giving them ideas.
6	(agrees)
4	Explain to them how to get the answer.
1	Trying to work it out with them.
8	If they are stuck on what the question means you can help them understand it.
6	That's what I was going to say!
7	Give them some methods to help them.
	How can your friends help you in the classroom?
1	By talking with them… Miss, that was from 1 and 2. **(Says 2 was going to say it).**
	Is this any sort of talking? What about football?
1	Talking about Maths or Literacy.
2	Talking about stuff that you don't want to hear.
5	If you are stuck on a question… they could like help you to get the answer but not tell you the answer. **(6 agrees – 1&2 support this too!)**
7	I think, if you help them with a question, and then you got stuck, they would help you back to say thank you.
8	The person that was helping you could tell you the way that they work it out and then you may be able to use it another time as well.
2	They could work it out with you.
12	If you get stuck on your work, do you ask the teacher a friend or both? 21:15
1	Teacher
2	Teacher.
3	Teacher.
4	Teacher.
5	Teacher.
6	Teacher.
7	Teacher.
8	Friend.
1	Sometimes I would have to ask both of them Miss.
2	So would I.
	So why would nearly all of you want to ask the teacher rather than a friend?
6	Because the teacher was the one who explained what you are supposed to be doing, so she can help you and explain other things to you.
8	I'd ask the friend first because if they explained it to you and I don't get it then I'd go and ask the teacher.
1	The friend could think that you know it but you don't and need to ask the teacher. **(4/ 6 agree)**
5	Sometimes you ask the teacher because like your friend might be wrong but the teacher is the one who explained it to you so she's probably got more chance of being right.
	How could the teacher help all the children in your class?
	She could tell one person and they could tell the rest of the class.
	She could stand up in the middle of the class and explain to all of us.
7	That's if one person asks, that's true. But that could mean she could have 26 things to explain. So
6	think, there could be one teacher and 26 children, they might be able to work the answer out between them.
	If you friend said she has got the answer to the question you would never know if you were right or wrong. **Would it be marked anyway?** What? **Your teacher would mark it.** What I'm trying to
8	say is, if your friend might give you the answer to the question, just to help yer, and then you never know if you are right or wrong so you should ask the teacher. **Oh I see, you are worried that if she gets it wrong you would get it wrong.** Yes.
	If there were two teachers there, the teacher could to the other teacher to go over and help the children.
	The assistant teacher.
2	I would ask the teacher first because my friend might get all mixed up.
	So you are worried that the teacher knows everything but your friends don't.
6	Miss, the teacher has sheets Miss showing them what to do.
3	**With the answers on?**
	Yes.
8	You ask the teacher because your friend might not have started the work yet.

8	If there were two teachers I would have split them into groups.
13	When people are talking how can you show you are listening?
2	Watch the teacher and be quiet.
6	Put your hand up and answer the teacher.
4	You could keep your eyes on the teacher to show that you're listening.
2	That's what I said!
3	You could her like by put your hand up and if you get the question wrong it shows you are still trying and she knows what you are doing.
7	Look at the teacher's board and listen to her… sit up.
8	Stay focused and concentrate.
6	Fold your arms and look.
	You have all talked about listening to your teacher and not your friend. Do you feel that is not as important to listen to each other?
2	Yes, you've got to listen to your friend and what they have to say but more importantly you have to listen to your teacher.
7	Because she helps you more.
3	Because your friends might not know what to do.
7	The friend might not have listened to the teacher. **(Talking to 3).**
7	The friend might not be focused on the teacher Miss.
6	The friend might not have listened to the teacher or watched the board.
2	You friend might be saying are we going to the baths or not but you could say be quiet and focus on the teacher because we've got something to learn here.
	What if your friend is taking to you about the work though? What if its your turn to tell the class how you have done your maths, wouldn't you like to tell them?
7	No.
	I think you probably would.
3	I would want them to know my opinion and then listen to theirs.
4	I don't get it?
6	I wouldn't because if you carry on you that means you will finish your work.
7	If you forget all the children that are messing you will be able to put your work down on paper.
14	If you are working in a group with other people how can you make sure it goes well? **30:20**
7	You could put your hands up and the teacher will go round everyone.
3	If you were working in a group on your table people could take turns like what they think the teacher has asked you a question and you could all choose which one is the best answer.
	That is what I was going to say. **That's 8 and 5**
5	**How can we make it better when we work all together?**
6	Miss, you could all discuss what you are going to do Miss, and… there might be two answers for one of the questions, one could put that answer for one of the questions and the other one after they have finished.
	So one could put one and one can put the other answer.
4	I would say in our class we all split up into five tables, you could start from one table and go round the class, to what people have for their answers, and their opinion.
	If you work in a group you could all share ideas.
8	You could go from one table to another and come back round to the first table, and go through all the people.
7	**So is there anything else you can think about, about what you like/don't like, about working on your own/in pairs. Is it easier to work together in some subjects than others?**
	I like working together, in groups in literacy
	It's easier for pairs in literacy because I think literacy is a bit confusing for me, and in maths, it's easier for me.
3	I like doing literacy with all the people on my table.
4	I like working in a group for literacy because I always get stuck on it, and just say everyone has got their own opinion and we would like think, which one is the best answer.
6	Miss, in literacy I like working on my own because we do all stories… I like the draft book.
3	I like working in groups on maths because sometimes I find some questions a little bit hard.
	In any subject I like working in a pair but in literacy I like working on my own.
	In literacy I like working on my own because… oh Miss, I forgot!
7	I like working in numeracy on my own or in a pair because if it's a hard lesson I like working in a pair because you get your own ideas and nobody else's but when you are just writing on a sheet,
6	like working on my own because I like to know my own answers.
5	In literacy I like working in a group because I'm not that really good at literacy and all the people on my table help me.

4 3	Because I think literacy is confusing, that I should just try and do it and use my other skills for writing drafts and all that.
	I like working on 'Here I am' by myself because
	What is it?
	RE Religious Education.
6	It's quite easy and you can do it on your own.
	So when you feel you can do something well, you prefer to do it on your own. But when
1	**you feel you will get stuck with things, you would rather work with somebody else.**
	Yes
3	I like working in a pair on geography. Because I don't really know nothing about the local area.
6	I think in science Miss, I would work in pairs because… if we work in pairs, like, if we learnt about forces, we could talk to each other and give each other ideas.
3	I like to work in pairs… because I like working with people and it's a good lesson, getting ideas of another person.
	I like working in pairs in maths because I'm not very good at maths.
All 1	I think in design and technology I like to work on my own when making things. We were making jam tarts this year, you don't really need someone to help yer make a jam tart do yer?
	I would, I'm hopeless at baking! (Laughter)
6	Miss, I like working on my own in history Miss because we do all good things in history, and every time I do something in history sometimes people interrupt.
4	I like working on my own in art because, when you are like art, and its something you really want to get on with, while other people are trying to help you do it, you're like, go away, I want to do it
6	by myself.
7	I want to get off this question. We've been on it about half an hour! **I agree!**
	Miss, I like working on my own in art because you could be doing something and another person could come over to yer and make you not do the lesson, and talk about something.
	I like working on my own in maths because sometimes on my table are quiet, sometimes.
All	I like working on my own in art because there is not a lot that you can really share in art.
1	I like working on my own in art because I find it easy.
8	I like working on my own in art because you can get away because I like drawing better than writing, a little bit.
	Is there anything else anyone would like to say before I switch the machine off?
6	Miss, I like working in 'Here I am' because when you are doing something that's good, like drawing things, you can get on with it and someone come over and start messing.
1	I like working on my own in geography as that's my favourite lesson because last time we went around the school. **Total time: 42:01**
15 and	If you have to work with someone would you like to choose yourself or are you happy for the teacher to choose? **Not asked because covered earlier.**
16	Is there any difference between working with one friend or lots of friends? **covered earlier.**

Children Interview Questions

Foundation	KS1	Lower KS2	Upper KS2 X

Disk 2 ~ Track 2	
1	How often do you work on your own?
1	2 or 3 times a week.
2	2 or 3 times a week.
3	I don't work on my own every day – 2 or 3 times a week.
4	Once a week.
5	2 or 3 times a week.
6	2 or 3 times a week.
7	2 or 3 times a week.
8	2 or 3 times a week.
2	How often do you work in pairs?
1	Every day.
2	Less than once a week.
3	Every day.
4	Every day.
5	Every day.
6	Every day.
7	Every day.
8	Every day.
3	How often do you work in groups?
1	Less than once a week.
2	Less than once a week.
3	2 or 3 times a week.
4	Less than once a week.
5	2 or 3 times a week.
6	Once a week.
7	Once a week.
8	Less than once a week.
4	What kind of speaking and listening activities have you done? It's base around you talking to people about your work.
5	I do in role play.
6	When we finish our work… try and ask our partner what we think of each others work.
	In maths when we are discussing the problem… on the carpet. (Another child agrees).
3	In maths when we were discussing answers to the problems.
1	Sometimes when we have finished our work we sit on the carpet and read our work out what
7	we've done. **(Another child agrees; 5 & 6 are the same)**
5	What do you like about speaking and listening activities?
1	Sharing ideas. That's what I was going to say! **(8 agrees)**
2	When we're reading a book.
3	When we read out everyone is looking at yer. **So you like that?** Yeah.
4	You find out what others think of your work.
6	When you listen to other people's literacy work.
7	**(Agrees with 1 and 8) 1, 7 and 8 - share ideas.**
6	Is there anything you don't like about speaking and listening?
6	When everyone looks at you.
8	When someone? is talking while you're reading it out.
5	When you make a mistake and everyone laughs at you. **That's not very kind. Does it happen a lot?** No
7	When you tell the teacher the answer and everyone else writes it down.
	Yeah… it's horrible that.
8	I like that!
4	When you read a book and you miss a line and everyone looks at yer.
7	Tell me if you prefer - reading, writing or speaking and listening?
8	Writing
7	Writing
6	Speaking and listening
5	Speaking and listening

4	Reading
3	Speaking and listening
2	Reading
1	Reading
8	People who like reading the best – what is it that you like reading the best?
3	Just like it. **No particular reason?** No
2	I like reading because I get into the story more… like something to do.
1	Because when people make films about the stories, the stories include more.
6	Like Harry Potter.
9	What about the two who preferred writing?
7	You don't have to discuss answers. **9:30**
8	When you write you can just write what you think instead of talking to everyone about it. So you can just write and show the teacher.
10	And our speaking and listeners?
6	Because when you are listening to the people it's showing you what they thought of the question and you're giving what you thought and you can discuss it and work out the best answer for the question.
5	You don't have to just write everything down, you can tell everyone what you've got and what they've got.
3	If you don't like speaking you can listen to other people's answers.
11	Is it more difficult to work on your own than with a friend?
	4 yes's , that means 4 no's.
12	What are the things you like or don't like about working on your own?
8	You can share answers, you can discuss things.
3	When you are stuck on an answer you've got another friend to help yer.
6	I would have said that.
5	So would I.
4	I like to work out the answer for myself.
13	What is good or bad about working with other children?
6	Say I get an answer, then on the next question I don't know the answer, but your partner does, then you get the answer. **(All agree)**
7	Say you know all the answers and the person you are working with doesn't have a clue then they just copy yer.
3	I don't like working in a group or a partner as we always end up arguing.
4	There's too much difference in opinion.
14	How can you help your friends in class?
2	Giving them ideas of how to do the work – they might not hear what the teacher said. Help them when they are stuck. **(Others agree with 2 and 8)**
15	How can your friends help you in class?
2	By giving you ideas but not just the answers.
8	Mines the same as 2 **(Others agree with 2 and 8)**
7	You want to work out the answer but they tell you the answer.
16	If you get stuck on your work, do you ask the teacher or a friend?
2	A teacher **Why?** Because the teachers are smarter. They give you the answers because they know more.
6	They lead you towards an answer.
8	You remember what the teacher told you to do.
1	You can ask a friend fist, but if they don't know the answer you can ask the teacher then.
4	I'd ask a friend because if they know the answer they can show you how they worked it out, so you would know how to do it next time. I'd ask a friend or a teacher. **(6 agrees)**
5	I'd ask the teacher because a friend could give you the answer but it could be wrong. **(8 supports**
7	**this)** The wrong answer.
3	I ask a friend then the teacher to see I my friend is right or the teacher is wrong.
17	When people are talking how can you show you are listening? **19:40**
2	By looking at them and answering them back if they say what do you recon about that? And they say, what part did you like the best you can just tell them.
8	Mine's the same as hers **(6 & 7 also agree)**
1	You know they are not listening because they are fidgeting and they have not got their arms folded and they are looking out of the window. (all others agree with 1)
18	If you are working in a group with other people how can you make sure it goes well?
3	Make sure each one in the group gets their say.

1	Make sure everyone agrees on it.
6	Make sure everyone checks their answers.
8	Make sure everyone explains their answer of how they got it right.
	(All others agree with 6)
19	If you are working in pairs or groups, what are the advantages or disadvantages?
6	In a group, there's more people to answer the question – if you don't know the answer, if you didn't know or your partner didn't know, there's bound to be someone in the group who knows. **(everyone else agrees) I want more than this.**
3	If you have got an answer and you ask the teacher, and they say, if your work is right and your mate has copied yer and they ask the teacher you will end up arguing. **(? Hard to understand)** There's more chances of getting your questions right in a group because there's more of you. **Any bad points of working in a group?**
6	Might not agree with the answers. **So what would you do then?** If you do not agree, then you go your way I'll go mine. **(4 agrees).**
7	I love working in pairs.
6	Good things, if you don't know an answer then your mate can help yer, and if they don't know an
8	answer you can help them, you can just give ideas, not just copying me.
2	You don't have to argue, you might do two answers. When you are in a pair instead of a group, I could do one question and answer it and your partner can do the other and answer it. **Divide the work up.**
8	If you didn't hear what the teacher said you could ask your partner, they might have heard and
6	they will tell yer, and show you how to do it.
1	The good thing about working in pairs, if you are in a group, like half the group might snide off, and they would know all the answers, they go off with all the answers. The teacher might put you with someone who is not your mate.
20	If you have to work with someone would you like to choose yourself or are you happy for the teacher to choose?
	(7 choose to pick themselves, one doesn't)
6	If you have an argument with them you end up boxing.
21	Is there anything else you can tell me about working on your own, with a partner or in a group?
5	I you are working with a partner, and the teacher chooses, you might get stuck with someone you don't like.
2	They might be silly and get you into trouble, and they blame you.
7	They could disturb you. **Total Time 27:45**

Notes from open-ended questions:
Teachers and *Support Staff (typed in italics)*

23	What are the positive and negative aspects of speaking and listening, for the teacher and for the children?

-ve: with a class that cannot settle, it is difficult for plenary; that environment (teacher); for pupils - they miss out on an activity that broadens their literacy skills; children not aware of the viewpoint of others and feelings of others.

-ve: At times difficult to manage as some children can become a little 'lively'. Some children, depending on the task or depending on who they are grouped with, find it difficult to communicate. They need lots of practice to become proficient.

-ve: more confident can lead the discussion but not allow others their voice.
+ve: allows children to discuss their ideas and also gives teacher the chance to re-direct any misunderstandings.

+ve: Children enjoy speaking and listening activities – they like to contribute to discussions (paired/group/class) They are able to think things through first before embarking on written tasks **thinking and collaborative skills** (ownership).
–ve: Some children can dominate/become passive. Teacher needs to be aware and balance/rebalance discussions etc. **teacher scaffolding and intervention only when necessary**

+ve: Children can benefit from others' experiences.
Teacher may learn things about quieter children who are unwilling to converse with adults.
-ve: Conversations can go off at a tangent. Children could just 'chat'. It could get noisy!

+ve: brings on children's confidence; discuss what work they've done with each other; solve problems
-ve: difficult to assess; sometimes with such a young age they chat about what they want.

+ve: Children who are often quiet or shy respond well to working with others.
-ve: 'Louder' children often drown out the quieter children. Assessing can be difficult.

+ve: Children can discuss things of interest to them and are more involved. For some children it is the one way they can get their ideas across, as they struggle with their writing. I can't see any negative aspects.

+ve: It helps quiet children to express their opinions; it encourages them to speak up; most benefit.
-ve: Loud children tend to take over; some children find it hard to speak and listen.

+ve: Brings their confidence out and learns them to discuss with each other.

+ve: Children try to speak together, learn take turns and listen to other people's ideas. May notice children interested in some topics more than others.

+ve: So they can understand the task and for me to pass on information correctly.

+ve for children: Children able to assist each others' learning via speaking and listening.
-ve for children: Not always good due to some children being incapable of listening to others.
+ve for teacher: Speaking and listening enables teacher to establish children's knowledge if they are not able to express themselves through writing.
-ve: for teacher: Though if valid points are made about a particular topic it is much harder to record evidence of knowledge.

24	**What are the benefits and disadvantages of children working collaboratively, for the teacher and for the children?**

Benefits to children: children learn to listen and respond to one another; they get to exchange ideas; they get to practice 'give and take'.
Benefits to teacher – blossoming of ideas.
Disadvantages for children: Some children find it difficult to work with others;
Disadvantages for teacher: keeping children on task.

-ve: Sometimes not a lot of work is completed.
+ve: Less confident children can be guided by their peers. **Peer scaffolding**

Benefits: Child's views/opinions can be reaffirmed by peers *** (Boost confidence to contribute) Activities are more 'hands on'/not too much sitting/listening – more interesting lessons. (Child view?)
Possible Disadvantages: Some children may not contribute and leave the work to others – teacher needs to be aware/keep track of this (problem sometimes)

+ve: Less confident children are supported by their peers. It can be easier to organise a group than a whole class in terms of time and resources. Combined knowledge may lead to better outcomes. **Mercer's work!**
 -ve: maybe over ruled by their peers also!

+ve: They are able to work collaboratively. Children do discuss work with each other and are able to understand it better.
-ve: Not all children can work collaboratively; poorer children just copy their work.

+ve: Children learn so much from each other. Class learn to listen rather than just speak.
-ve: Some children never learn to listen; it is a hard skill to achieve.

+ve: Some children grow in confidence when they work together and they enjoy sharing ideas and presenting something to the class.
-ve: However, sometimes children prefer in my class to work on their own, so they don't join in as much.

-ve: Some children can work collaboratively but the poor group would just copy off each other.

ve: Quiet children may go unnoticed because of loud chatter; some children may dominate conversation.

+ve: Ideas pooled together stretch others' imagination.

+ve: Children are able to come up with things that they may not have thought of on their own. Possibility of more actual written work being recorded 'two head better than one' idea **Mercer again**
-ve: chances of copying increased. Children with limited knowledge may end up going with the flow of everyone else.

Please use the space below for any other comments.

I have been doing lots of work using philosophical enquiry with my class and other year groups. I feel this helps the children really <u>listen</u> to each other and consider others' ideas. It also helps the child express their thoughts and feelings in words.

The learning environment/classroom can dictate the success/failure of collaborative activities ie – smaller classrooms – hinders group/collaborative activities. All primary classrooms should be 'organised' like the Foundation Stage classrooms – if we had space!

This made me think! With younger children it is generally accepted that lots of chatter goes on. Young children need an extensive vocabulary before they can learn to read or write successfully **Hohmann**

Each child needs to be guided to find best way of learning for them.

Qu 23: What are the positive and negative aspects of speaking and listening, for the teacher and for the children?

Negatives for the teacher:
- With a class that cannot settle, it is difficult for plenary.
- At times difficult to manage as some children can become a little 'lively'.
- Conversations can go off at a tangent. Children could just 'chat' about what they want (2).
- It could get noisy!
- Difficult to assess (2) *Though valid points are made about a particular topic it is much harder to record evidence of knowledge.*

Positives for the teacher:
- Gives teacher the chance to re-direct any misunderstandings.
- Teacher may learn things about quieter children who are unwilling to converse with adults.
- *May notice children interested in some topics more than others.*
- *So they can understand the task and for me to pass on information correctly.*
- *Speaking and listening enables teacher to establish children's knowledge if they are not able to express themselves through writing.*

Negatives for the children:
- For pupils - they miss out on an activity that broadens their literacy skills.
- Children not aware of the viewpoint of others and feelings of others.
- Some children, depending on the task or depending on who they are grouped with, find it difficult to communicate. They need lots of practice to become proficient.
- More confident can lead the discussion but not allow others their voice.
- Some children can dominate/become passive. Teacher needs to be aware and balance/rebalance discussions etc. **teacher scaffolding and intervention only when necessary.**
- Louder' children often drown out the quieter children. **Loud children tend to take over.**
- *Some children find it hard to speak and listen.*
- *Not always good due to some children being incapable of listening to others.*

Positives for the children:
- Allows children to discuss their ideas.
- Children enjoy speaking and listening activities.
- Children like to contribute to discussions (paired/group/class).
- They are able to think things through first before embarking on written tasks **thinking and collaborative skills** (ownership).
- Children can benefit from others' experiences.
- Brings on children's confidence. *Brings their confidence out.*
- Discuss what work they've done with each other; *and learns them [sic] to discuss with each other.*
- Solve problems.
- Children who are often quiet or shy respond well to working with others. *It helps quiet children to express their opinions; it encourages them to speak up.*
- Children can discuss things of interest to them and are more involved.
- For some children it is the one way they can get their ideas across, as they struggle with their writing. I can't see any negative aspects.
- *Children try to speak together, learn take turns and listen to other people's ideas.*
- *Children able to assist each others' learning via speaking and listening.*

Qu 24: What are the benefits and disadvantages of children working collaboratively, for the teacher and for the children?

Negatives for the teacher:
- Difficulty keeping children on task.
- Sometimes not a lot of work is completed.
- Some children may not contribute and leave the work to others – teacher needs to be aware/keep track of this (problem sometimes).
- *Chances of copying increased. Children with limited knowledge may end up going with the flow of everyone else.*

Positives for the teacher:
- Blossoming of ideas.
- It can be easier to organise a group than a whole class in terms of time and resources.
- *Possibility of more actual written work being recorded 'two head better than one' idea.* **Mercer again.**

Negatives for the children:
- Some children find it difficult to work with others.
- Less confident children maybe over ruled by their peers.
- Not all children can work collaboratively.
- Poorer children just copy others' work *(2)*.
- Some children never learn to listen; it is a hard skill to achieve.
- Sometimes children prefer to work on their own, so they don't join in as much.
- *Quiet children may go unnoticed because of loud chatter.*
- *Some children may dominate conversation.*

Positives for the children:
- Children learn to listen and respond to one another.
- They get to exchange ideas.
- They get to practice 'give and take'.
- Less confident children can be guided/supported by their peers (2). **Peer scaffolding.**
- Child's views/opinions can be reaffirmed by peers. *** (Boost confidence to contribute).
- Activities are more 'hands on'/not too much sitting/listening – more interesting lessons. (Child view?).
- Combined knowledge may lead to better outcomes. **Mercer's work!**
- They are able to work collaboratively.
- Children do discuss work with each other and are able to understand it better.
- Children learn so much from each other.
- Class learn to listen rather than just speak.
- Some children grow in confidence when they work together and they enjoy sharing ideas and presenting something to the class.
- *Ideas pooled together stretch others' imagination.*
- *Children are able to come up with things that they may not have thought of on their own.*

E1 Children's Questionnaire Questions

How do you prefer to work in class, most of the time?		
Nursery	19 responses	
* Please note, the child may have given more than one reason for their preference, or none at all, therefore the tally for reasons may differ from the total number given for preferred way of working.		
Reasons expressed for preference.		
I prefer to work on my own	26%	5*
• Because I like working on my own		2
• Because it's my job when I'm on my own. Now I'm four I don't work with a friend. When I was three I needed to work with a friend because I needed someone to help me.		2
• If I do my own work and no one sits by me it's good.		1
• Because it's all quiet.		1
I prefer to work in a pair	32%	6*
• Because it says so (instruction on wall, '2 can play in the water').		1
• I need a friend to help me.		1
• No reason given.		1
• I like to play with a friend.		2
• Because it's fun.		1
I prefer to work in a group	42%	8*
• I like to play with my friends.		4
• Because my Mum's got loads of children.		1
• Because my Mum told me to.		1
• No reason given.		3

How do you prefer to work in class, most of the time?		
Reception	20 responses	
* Please note, the child may have given more than one reason for their preference, or none at all, therefore the tally for reasons may differ from the total number given for preferred way of working.		
Reasons expressed for preference.		
I prefer to work on my own	25%	5*
• Because I like working on my own.		3
• To get my work done quicker.		1
• Because I want to get clever and read my book.		1
I prefer to work in a pair	45%	9*
• Groups are too noisy and I can't do my work.		1
• I don't like working on my own.		1
• No reason given.		1
• Because I like to work with a friend/we can work with each other.		4
• Because I get stuck/I need help.		3
I prefer to work in a group	30%	6*
• I like to be with my friends.		1
• Because they can help me.		1
• No reason given.		1
• Because we can share (the glue)		1
• Because it's good in a group.		1
• Because I want to.		1

How do you prefer to work in class, most of the time?		
Year 1	23 responses	
Please note, the child may have given more than one reason for their preference, or none at all, therefore the tally for reasons may differ from the total number given for preferred way of working.		
Reasons expressed for preference.		
I prefer to work on my own	17%	4*
• To get on with my work/to get my work done quicker.		3
• So there's nobody to talk to.		1
I prefer to work in a pair	44%	10*
• Because they tell you what to do/help me.		3
• To help each other/we can discuss things.		2
• It's easier.		1
• It's fun.		1
• Because they are nice to me.		1
• So we don't get shouted at.		1
I prefer to work in a group	39%	9*
• If I am stuck, they can help me/because you can ask people the answers.		3
• Because you work better.		1
• To help each other/because we can share work/we get to talk about it.		4
• Because it's easier.		1

How do you prefer to work in class, most of the time?		
Year 2	19 responses	
Please note, the child may have given more than one reason for their preference, or none at all, therefore the tally for reasons may differ from the total number given for preferred way of working.		
Reasons expressed for preference.		
I prefer to work on my own	32%	6*
• Because I can concentrate more.		3
• Because I think of good ideas myself.		2
• Because I can have peace and quiet.		3
I prefer to work in a pair	36%	7*
• Because they help you/give me ideas/partner helps you lots/because some people understand and I don't.		4
• Because I get mixed up so we can help each other/talk or whisper to the person next to you.		3
• I enjoy working with them.		2
I prefer to work in a group	32%	6*
• If I get stuck, I can ask someone in my group/they give me ideas.		2
• I like working in a group.		1
• You get more help and we can help each other.		3
• Because it's fun.		1

How do you prefer to work in class, most of the time?		
Year 3	23 responses	
Please note, the child may have given more than one reason for their preference, or none at all, therefore the tally for reasons may differ from the total number given for preferred way of working.		
Reasons expressed for preference.		
I prefer to work on my own	44%	10*
• Because it's good when no one distracts me.		1
• I can work faster.		3
• Because I can be quiet.		1
• I don't like people copying me.		1
• I don't like people leaning on me.		1
• It's much better.		1
• I like to get my own work done/your friend doesn't ask you what to do.		2
I prefer to work in a pair	56%	13*
• I want to work with a friend because when I am stuck they can help me/the work is hard		3
• No one distracts us.		1
• Because he will help me and I will help him/I like sharing my ideas/help each other.		3
• Because we get on well with each other/ you get to work with your best mate.		5
• Because I can work with a friend - I don't like to be on my own.		1
• Because a group is more noisy.		1
• Because if you work in a group, half of them switch off.		1
I prefer to work in a group	0%	0*

How do you prefer to work in class, most of the time?		
Year 4	21 responses	
Please note, the child may have given more than one reason for their preference, or none at all, therefore the tally for reasons may differ from the total number given for preferred way of working.		
Reasons expressed for preference.		
I prefer to work on my own	33%	7*
• Because in a group everyone shouts and it puts you off/is shouting at you when you try to say something.		2
• Because everyone gets me to talk and then I can't do it.		1
• I get more work done on my own.		2
• I can use my own ideas/get my own answers what I think.		2
• Because I end up moaning at people when they think they're right but I think they're wrong.		1
• I like working by myself because different people work in different ways.		1
I prefer to work in a pair	24%	5*
• I like to work in a pair because your partner can help you when you get stuck/ I get confused sometimes/sometimes I struggle on my own and I ask for help.		3
• Because you get help off the other person and you'll help them.		1
• Because a group is too loud and on my own is too hard.		1
I prefer to work in a group	43%	9*
• I like working in a group because we can share each other's ideas/because if you get stuck you have the rest of the group to help you work it out/work together to get the answer/talk about it.		8
• It's better to work in a group as it is easy.		1

How do you prefer to work in class, most of the time?		
Year 5	19 responses	
* Please note, the child may have given more than one reason for their preference, or none at all, therefore the tally for reasons may differ from the total number given.		
Reasons expressed for preference.		
I prefer to work on my own	5%	1 *
• Because in a group we always fall out.		1
• Because you can work faster.		1
• If I work with partners I'm always determined to copy off them.		1
• If I work on my own I learn more by my mistakes.		1
I prefer to work in a pair	74%	14 *
• Sometimes I'm not sure about the work, the person that I'm working with helps me.		1
• Because it's easier than a group and on your own.		1
• In a group you fight/argue/disagree/too many differences in opinion.		6
• Because I can get in a pair and work quieter/faster, it is easier to get down to work.		4
• Because in a pair we can both help each other/more ideas to share/talk so much/help each other when one does not understand.		6
• Because in a group there is a lot of chatting/too noisy.		2
• Because I talk too much in a group.		1
• A group is too crowded and it's quite hard to ask for help.		1
• Because if it was on my own it would be hard.		3
I prefer to work in a group	21%	4 *
• I like working in a group because we talk about work/get to share your questions/because if you get stuck you have the rest of the group to get the answer.		3
• No reason given.		

How do you prefer to work in class, most of the time?		
Year 6	22 responses	
* Please note, the child may have given more than one reason for their preference, or none at all, therefore the tally for reasons may differ from the total number given.		
Reasons expressed for preference.		
I prefer to work on my own	9%	2 *
• If you work on your own, you are not giving them any of your answers.		1
• You can work quicker and do work without being annoyed by other people.		1
I prefer to work in a pair	55%	12 *
• In a pair is better because I am not on my own.		1
• In a group everybody takes your answers.		2
• In a group most people start talking.		1
• Because in a pair you work quicker.		2
• Because in a pair we can help each other and discuss our answers/ share our ideas/talk about your answer		8
• It is easier to work with someone you know.		1
• Because when you are on your own with one friend it is quieter and you can concentrate better on your work.		1
• Because you get more work and more answers.		1
• You can sit with your best friend.		1
I prefer to work in a group	36%	8 *
• Because you can discuss your answers/because in a group you exchange all your answers and see which one is the best out of all/more people to discuss your answers with/get more ideas to put in your head.		8
• It's good to work together, it helps you to get along and listen to other people.		1

E2 Teacher and Support Staff Questionnaire

Results from Teacher and Support Staff Questionnaire.

Teachers ~ 8   TA/NNEB/Support Staff ~ 7

#	Statement	Agree strongly		Agree		Disagree		Disagree strongly	
1	Speaking and listening are just as important as reading and writing.	6	6	2	1				
2	Speaking and listening are vital to promote reading and writing.	6	6	2	1				
3	Speaking and listening activities are difficult to manage. No response - 1		1	6	3	2	2		
4	Children enjoy speaking and listening activities.	4	1	3	6	1			
5	Children prefer to work in pairs or groups, rather than on their own.	2	3	4	4	2			
6	I would prefer children to work independently.			2	3	5	4	1	
7	Children mess about during speaking and listening activities.			4	3	3	4	1	
8	Children benefit from working collaboratively with their peers.	4	4	4	3				
9	Children complete tasks better when they work with others. No response - 1	1	1	4	5	2	1		
10	I have seen children supporting each others' learning.	6	4	2	1				
11	I have received enough training for promoting speaking and listening.			1	4	7	3		
12	I would like to receive more training for promoting speaking and listening.	6	2	1	5			1	
13	I have a range of resources for promoting speaking and listening. No response - 1			3	3	5	2		1
14	I plan specifically for speaking and listening activities. No response - 1	2	2	5	4	1			
15	I only teach speaking and listening in literacy. No response - 1				1	4	3	4	2
16	I teach speaking and listening in many curricular subjects. No response - 1	4	4	4	2				
17	I encourage the children to work in pairs.	3	4	5	3				
18	I encourage the children to work in groups.	4	4	4	3				
19	Children still record their work individually even if they do a task in groups. No response - 1	2	3	4	1	2	2		
20	I find speaking and listening difficult to assess. No response - 1		1	7	2	1	3		

* No response given.

#	Statement	Every lesson		Every day		2 or 3 times a week		Once a week		Less than weekly	
21	How often do you allow children to work in pairs? **	3	3	3	1	1	1		1		
22	How often do you allow children to work in groups? *	2	3	5	2					1	1

162

Bibliography

Alexander, R. (2000) 'Sociocultural approach: teacher-student interaction in different cultural contexts' in Lillis, T. and McKinney, C. (2003) *Analysing language in context: a student workbook*, Stoke on Trent, Trentham Books Ltd.

Alexander, R. (n.d.) 'Talk in teaching and learning: international perspectives.' (in QCA, 2003c) *New perspectives on spoken English in the classroom: Discussion Papers.* Suffolk: QCA pp. 27-37

Bartlett, S., Burton, D. and Peim, N. (2001) *Introduction to Education Studies,* London: Paul Chapman Publishing

Bell, J. (1999) *Doing Your Research Project: A Guide for First-Time Researchers in Education and Social Science*, Third Edition, Buckingham: Open University Press

Black, P. and Wiliam, D (1998) *Inside the Black Box: Raising Standards through Classroom Assessment.* London: School of Education, King's College

Blum-Kulka, S. and Snow, C. (2004) 'Introduction: the potential of peer talk.' *Discourse Studies*, Aug2004, Vol. 6 (3), pp.291-307 (*AN 14197435*) EBSCO, *Electronic Journals*: [online] Liverpool: Liverpool John Moores University, Learning Services. Available at: http://weblinks2.epnet.com-EBSCOhost [Accessed 25th July 2005]

Blum-Kulka, S. and Huck-Taglicht, D. (2004) 'The social and discursive spectrum of peer talk.' *Discourse Studies*, Aug2004, Vol. 6 (3), pp.307-329 EBSCO, *Electronic Journals*: [online] Liverpool: Liverpool John Moores University, Learning Services. Available at: http://weblinks2.epnet.com-EBSCOhost [Accessed 25th July 2005]

Brown and Palinscar (1985) cited by North Central Regional Educational Laboratory: Excerpted from *What Is the Collaborative Classroom?* [online] Available at: http://www.ncrel.org/sdrs/areas/issues/students/learning/lr1pali.htm [Accessed 31st July 2005]

Buckley, B. (2003) *An investigation into the opportunities for peer group talk in the classroom,* (secondary age pupils). MA small-scale research project, Open University

Cameron, D. (n.d.) 'Schooling spoken language: beyond 'communication'?.' (in QCA, 2003c) *New perspectives on spoken English in the classroom: Discussion Papers.* Suffolk: QCA pp. 64-72

Cohen, L., and Manion, L. (1980) *Research Methods in Education*, London: Routledge

Cohen, L. and Manion, L. (1989) *A Guide to Teaching Practice,* London, Routledge

Cohen, L., Manion, L. & Morrison, K. (2000), *Research Methods in Education,* 5th ed. London: Routledge

Corden, R. (2000) *Literacy and Learning Through Talk*, Buckingham: Open University Press

Cotton, J. (1995) *The Theory of Learning*, London, Kogan Page

Coulthard, M. (2002) 'Forensic discourse analysis.' in Coulthard, M. (ed.) (2002) *Advances in spoken discourse analysis* [electronic resource] London; New York: Routledge [on line] Liverpool: Liverpool John Moores University, Learning Services. Available at: http://www.netLibrary.com/urlapi.asp?action=summary&v=1&bookid=70389 [Accessed 30th July 2005]

Czerniewska, P. (1992) *Learning about writing,* Oxford, Blackwell.

Dawes, L. and Wegerif, R. (1998) *Encouraging exploratory talk: practical suggestions.* This article first appeared in MAPE focus on Literacy Autumn 1998 [online] Available at:www.mape.org.uk/curriculum/english/exploratory.htm [Accessed 19th July 2005]

Denscombe, M. (1998), *The Good Research Guide*, Buckingham: Open University Press

Densombe, M. (2002), *Ground Rules for Good Research*, Buckingham: Open University Press

DfEE (1998) *The National Literacy Strategy: Framework for Teaching.* London: DfEE

DfEE (1999a) *The National Numeracy Strategy: Framework for Teaching Mathematics from Reception to Year 6.* Suffolk: DfEE

DfEE (1999b) *The National Curriculum: Handbook for Primary Teachers in England Key Stages 1 and 2.* London: DfEE

DfES (2003a) *Every Child Matters*, [online] Available at: www.everychildmatters.gov.uk/ [Accessed 19th July 2005]

DfES (2003b) *Excellence and Enjoyment: A Strategy for Primary Schools* Nottingham: DfES

DfES (2006) *Primary Framework for literacy and mathematics.* DfES.

(DfES 2007) *The Early Years Foundation Stage* Nottingham: DfES

Edwards, T. (n.d.) 'Purposes and characteristics of whole-class dialogue.' (in QCA, 2003c) *New perspectives on spoken English in the classroom: Discussion Papers.* Suffolk: QCA pp. 38-40

Ely, R., Gleason, J. and McCabe, A. (1996) '"Why Didn't You Talk to Your Mommy, Honey?": Parents' and Children's Talk.' *Research on Language and Social Interaction,* Vol. 29 (1), pp.7-25 EBSCO, *Electronic Journals*: [online] Liverpool: Liverpool John Moores University, Learning Services. Available at: http://web11.epnet.com/resultlist. [Accessed 26th July 2005]

ESRC (nd) *Using Talk to Activate Learners' Knowledge,* [online] Available at: www.ex.ac.uk/~damyhill/talk/BPRS.htm [Accessed 19th July 2005]

Fontana, D. (1992) *Psychology for Teachers,* Leicester, The British Psychological Society

Fox, R. (2005) *Teaching and Learning Lessons from Psychology*, Oxford: Blackwell Publishing

Francis, G. and Hunston, S. (1998) 'Analysing everyday conversation.' in Coulthard, M. (ed.) (2002) *Advances in spoken discourse analysis* [electronic resource] London ; New York : Routledge [on line] Liverpool: Liverpool John Moores University, Learning Services. Available at: http://www.netLibrary.com/urlapi.asp?action=summary&v=1&bookid=70389 [Accessed 30th July 2005]

Galton, M. (n.d.) 'Learning to think through conversation.' (in QCA, 2003c) *New perspectives on spoken English in the classroom: Discussion Papers.* Suffolk: QCA pp. 48-51

Gibbs, G. (1994) *Learning in Teams: A Student Manual,* Oxford: Oxford Centre for Staff Development

Gibbs, G. and Habeshaw, T. (1989) *Preparing to teach – An introduction to effective teaching in higher education,* Bristol, Technical and Educational Services Limited

Godinho, S. and Shrimpton, B. (2002) The University of Melbourne Conference, December 2002, *Exploring Differences in Students' Engagement in Literature Discussions.* [online] Available at: www.aare.edu.au/02pap/god02471.htm [Accessed 25th July 2005]

Goodman, S., Lillis. T., Maybin, J. and Mercer, N. (2003) *Language, Literacy and Education: A Reader*, Stoke on Trent, Trentham Books Ltd

Gustafson, B. and MacDonald, D. (2004) 'Talk as a Tool for Thinking: Using Professional Discourse Practices to Frame Children's Design-Technology Talk.' *Canadian Journal of Science, Mathematics, & Technology Education*, Jul2004, Vol. 4 (3), pp.331-352 (*AN 14373138*) EBSCO, *Electronic Journals*: [online] Liverpool: Liverpool John Moores University, Learning Services. Available at: http://weblinks2.epnet.com-EBSCOhost [Accessed 25th July 2005]

Grugeon, E., Hubbard, L., Smith, C., and Dawes L. (2001) *Teaching Speaking and Listening in the Primary School,* 2nd ed. London: David Fulton

Hall, J. (February 2005) *A review of the contribution of brain science to teaching and learning* [Executive Summary of Neuroscience and Education, online] Available at: www.scre.ac.uk [Accessed 19th July 2005]

Harmon, J. (2002) 'Teaching independent word learning strategies to struggling readers.' *Journal of Adolescent & Adult Literacy,* Apr2002, Vol. 45 (7), pp.606-616 EBSCO, *Electronic Journals*: [online] Liverpool: Liverpool John Moores University, Learning Services. Available at: http://search.epnet.com/login.aspx?direct=true&db=aph&an=7194725 [Accessed 26th July 2005]

Hicks, D. (1995) 'Discourse, teaching and learning' in Goodman, S., Lillis. T., Maybin, J. and Mercer, N. (2003) *Language, Literacy and Education: A Reader*, Stoke on Trent, Trentham Books Ltd

Hohmann, M. (2005), Listening to Language and Literacy. National High/Scope UK Conference, University of Manchester, 25th June 2005. *A Sensory-Motor Approach to Language and Literacy for Children Under Three.*

Horizon, 'The origins of Thinking, Language and Art.' UK, BBC2, Feb 20th 2003

Ivanicõ, R. (2003) 'Interview with Roz Ivanicõ', E844 *Language and Literacy in a Changing World* [AUDIO CD], CDA5240, The Open University Press.

Jaques, D. (2000) *Learning in Groups,* London: Kogan Page

Jefferson, G. (1984) 'Transcription Notation' in Atkinson, J. M. and Heritage, J. (eds.) (1984) *Structures of social action: Studies in conversation analysis* (pp.ix–xviii) London: Cambridge University Press

Kuhn, T. S. (1970), *The Structure of Scientific Revolutions,* 2nd ed. Chicago: University of Chicago Press

Leonard, L. & Leonard, P. (2003, September 17). 'The continuing trouble with collaboration: Teachers talk'. *Current Issues in Education* [On-line], 6(15). Available at: http://cie.ed.asu.edu/volume6/number15/ [Accessed 27th April 2005]

Lillis, T. and McKinney, C. (2003) *Analysing language in context: a student workbook*, Stoke on Trent: Trentham Books

Machado de Almeida Mattos, A. (2000) 'A Vygotskian approach to evaluation in foreign language learning contexts' in Goodman, S., Lillis. T.,

Maybin, J. and Mercer, N. (2003) *Language, Literacy and Education: A Reader*, Stoke on Trent: Trentham Books

Maybin, J. (2003) 'Voices, intertextuality and induction into schooling' in Goodman, S., Lillis. T., Maybin, J. and Mercer, N. (2003) *Language, Literacy and Education: A Reader*, Stoke on Trent, Trentham Books Ltd Chapter 11: pp159-170

Maybin, J. (n.d.) '"What's the hottest part of the sun? Page 3!" Children's exploration of adolescent gender identities through informal talk.'
(in QCA, 2003c) *New perspectives on spoken English in the classroom: Discussion Papers.* Suffolk: QCA pp. 41-47

Mayer, R. (2002, 2003) cited in WikEd [online]
http://moodle.ed.uiuc.edu/wiked/index.php/Reciprocal_teaching
[Accessed 31st July 2005]

McClelland, N. (2002) *Talk tall* [online] Available at:
www.literacytrust.org.uk This article appears in the September 2002 issue of *Literacy Today* (issue number 32).

McNiff, J., Lomax, P. & Whitehead, J. (1996), *You and Your Action Research Project*, London: Routledge

Mercer, N. (2000) *Words and Minds: how we use language to think together*, London: Routledge

Mercer, N. (n.d.) 'The educational value of 'dialogic talk' in 'whole-class dialogue'.' (in QCA, 2003c) *New perspectives on spoken English in the classroom: Discussion Papers.* Suffolk: QCA pp. 73-76

Mercer, N., Wegerif, R. and Dawes, L. (1999) 'Children's Talk and the Development of Reasoning in the Classroom.' *British Educational Research Journal*, Feb99, Vol. 25 (1), pp.95-112 (*AN 1784491*) EBSCO, *Electronic Journals*: [online] Liverpool: Liverpool John Moores University, Learning Services. Available at: http://weblinks2.epnet.com-EBSCOhost
[Accessed 25th July 2005]

Myhill, D. (nd) *Talk, Talk, Talk: Teaching and Learning in Whole Class Discourse* [online] University of Exeter. Available at:
www.ex.ac.uk/~damyhill/talk/ [Accessed 19th July 2005]

National Literacy Trust [online] Available at: www.literacytrust.org.uk
[Accessed 19th July 2005]

QCA (2000a) *Curriculum Guidance for the Foundation Stage.* London: DfEE

QCA (2003b) *Speaking, Listening, Learning: working with children in Key Stages 1 and 2.* Nottingham: DfES

QCA (2003c) *New perspectives on spoken English in the classroom: Discussion Papers.* Suffolk: QCA

Research Methods in Education (2001), Handbook: Masters Programme in Education, Milton Keynes: Open University Press

Rojas-Drummond, S. (2000) 'Guided participation, discourse and the contribution of knowledge in Mexican classrooms' in Goodman, S., Lillis. T., Maybin, J. and Mercer, N. (2003) *Language, Literacy and Education: A Reader*, Stoke on Trent: Trentham Books

Shattuck, R. (1981) *The Forbidden Experiment: The Story of the Wild Boy of Aveyron,* London, Quartet Books Ltd.

Simpson, M. & Tuson, J. (1995) *Using Observations in Small-Scale Research,* Edinburgh: The Scottish Council for Research in Education

Sinclair, J. and Coulthard, M. (1975) 'Towards an analysis of discourse' in Coulthard, M. (ed.) (2002) *Advances in spoken discourse analysis* [electronic resource] London ; New York : Routledge [on line] Liverpool: Liverpool John Moores University, Learning Services. Available at: http://www.netLibrary.com/urlapi.asp?action=summary&v=1&bookid=70389 [Accessed 30th July 2005]

Sinclair, J. (2002) 'Priorities in discourse analysis' in Coulthard, M. (ed.) (2002) *Advances in spoken discourse analysis* [electronic resource] London ; New York: Routledge [on line] Liverpool: Liverpool John Moores University, Learning Services. Available at: http://www.netLibrary.com/urlapi.asp?action=summary&v=1&bookid=70389 [Accessed 30th July 2005]

Stewart, M. (2004) 'Learning through research: an introduction to the main theories of learning.' *Learning and Teaching Press.* Spring 2004, vol.4 (1), pp. 6-14 Liverpool: Liverpool John Moores University, Learning Development Unit

Sullivan, A. (2002) International Education Research Conference. Australian Association for Research in Education, Brisbane, Australia 2002, *Enhancing peer culture in a primary school classroom* (pp.1-17) Curtin University of Technology [online] Available at: www.aare.edu.au/02pap/sul02200.htm [Accessed 25th July 2005]

SureStart [online] Available at: www.surestart.gov.uk/ [Accessed 19th July 2005]

Tilstone, C. (ed.) (1998) *Observing Teaching and Learning: Principles and Practice,* London: David Fulton Publishers

Torrance, H. and Pryor, J. (1998) 'Classroom assessment and the language of teaching' in Goodman, S., Lillis. T., Maybin, J. and Mercer, N. (2003) *Language, Literacy and Education: A Reader*, Stoke on Trent, Trentham Books Ltd

Wray, D. and Lewis, M. (2005) *From learning to teaching: Towards a model of teaching literacy* [online] Available at:
www.warwick.ac.uk/staff/D.J.Wray/Articles/teach.html
[Accessed 19th July 2005]

Wyse, D. and Jones, R. (2001) *Teaching English, Language and Literacy,* London: RoutledgeFalmer

~ end ~